Dear reader

We would like to express our sincere gratitude for your decision to purchase this book. It is an honor for us to share this work with you. We hope it can provide you with knowledge, inspiration and moments of leisure. Welcome to this journey of learning and discovery.

Yours sincerely,

DiMarko

Di Marko
2024

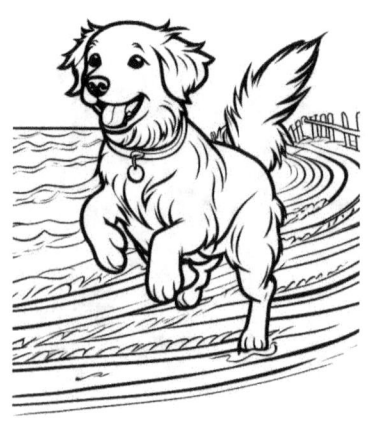
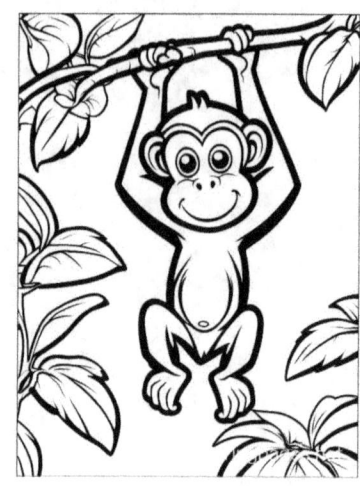

This Book Belongs to:

_____

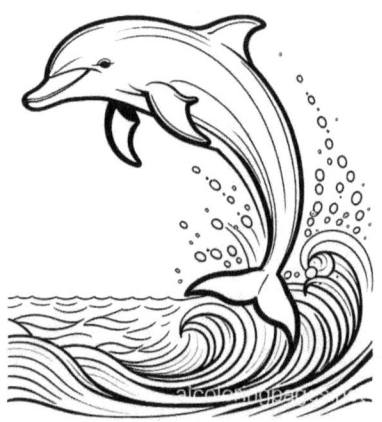
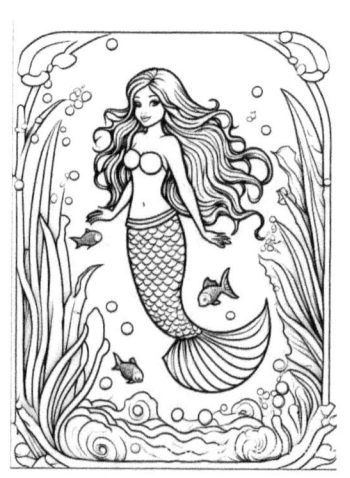

ALL RIGHTS RESERVED
2024

No part of this publication may be reproduced, distributed, or transmitted in any form or by any means, including photocopying, recording, or other electronic or mechanical methods, without the prior written permission of the publisher, except for brief quotations incorporated in critical reviews and other specific noncommercial uses. Any unauthorized replica of this work is prohibited.

©Di Marko publications
2024

Test Color Page

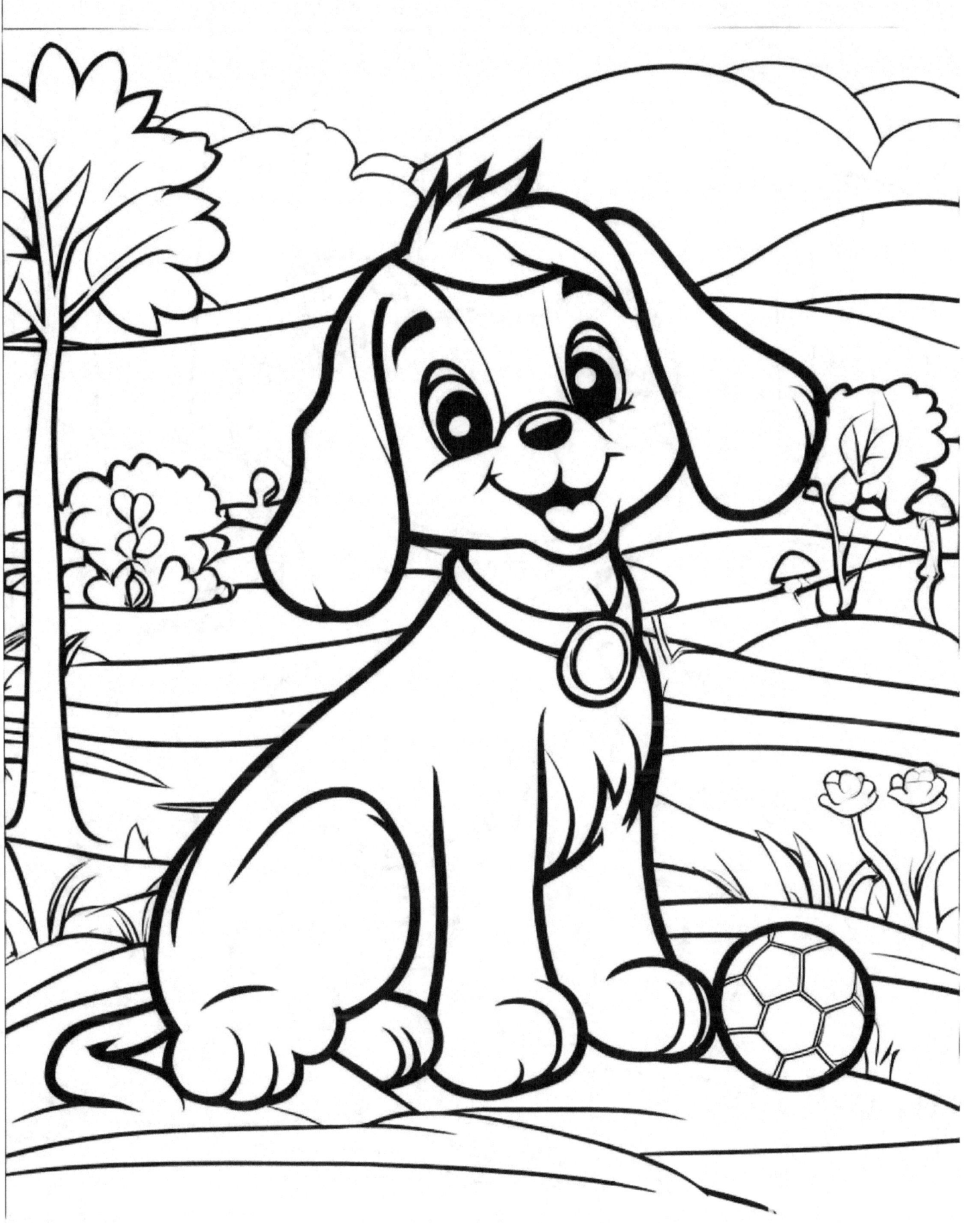

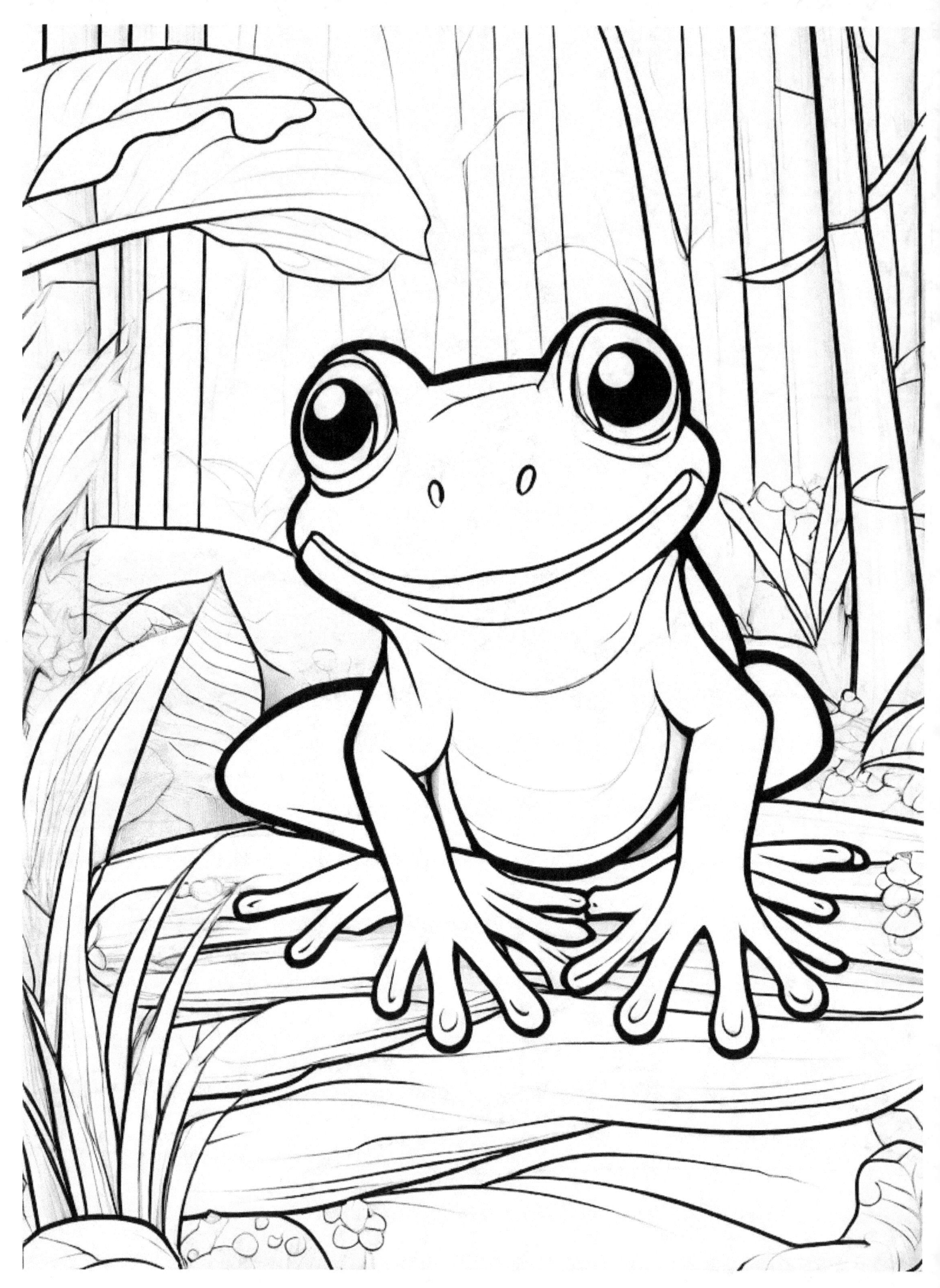

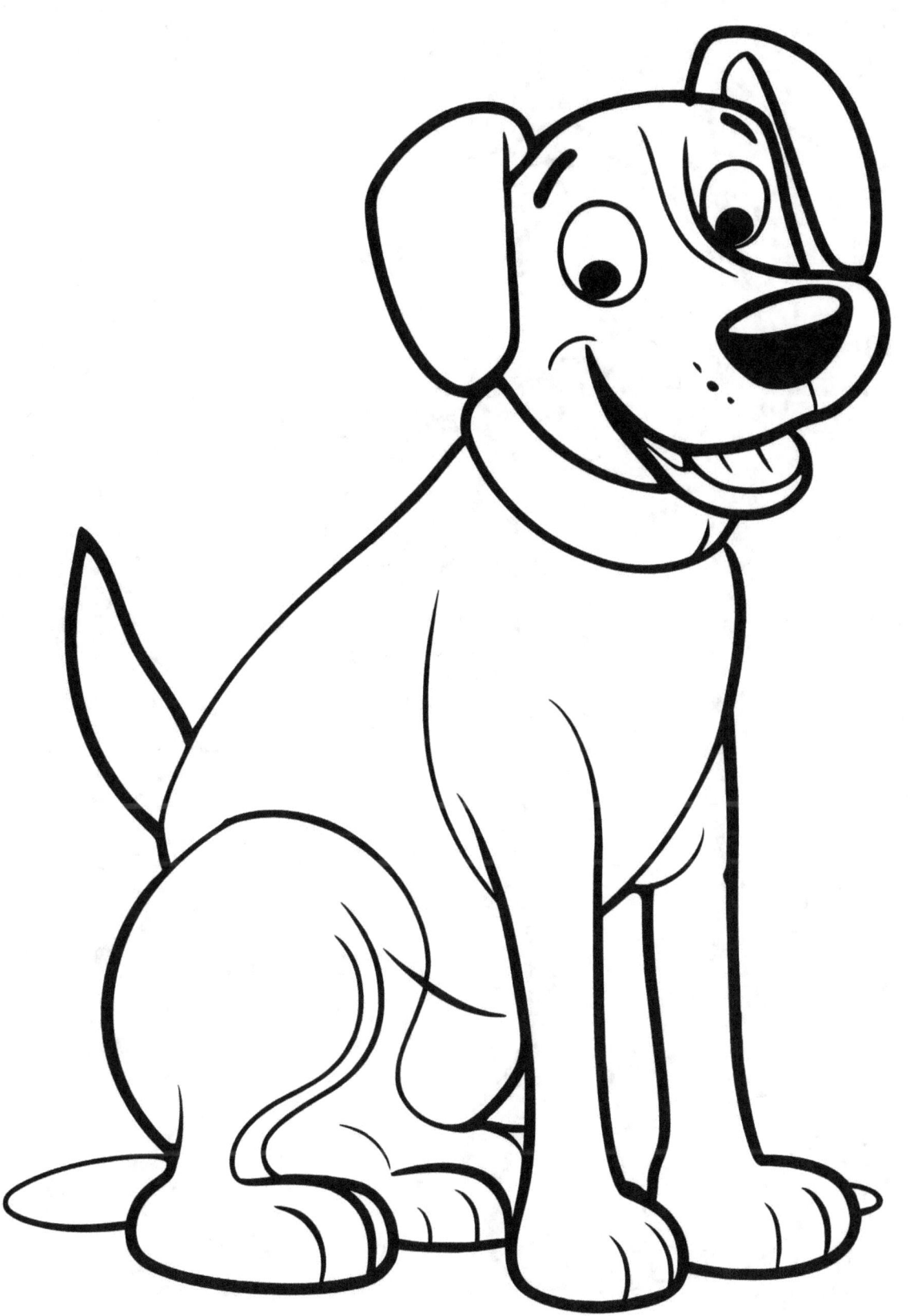

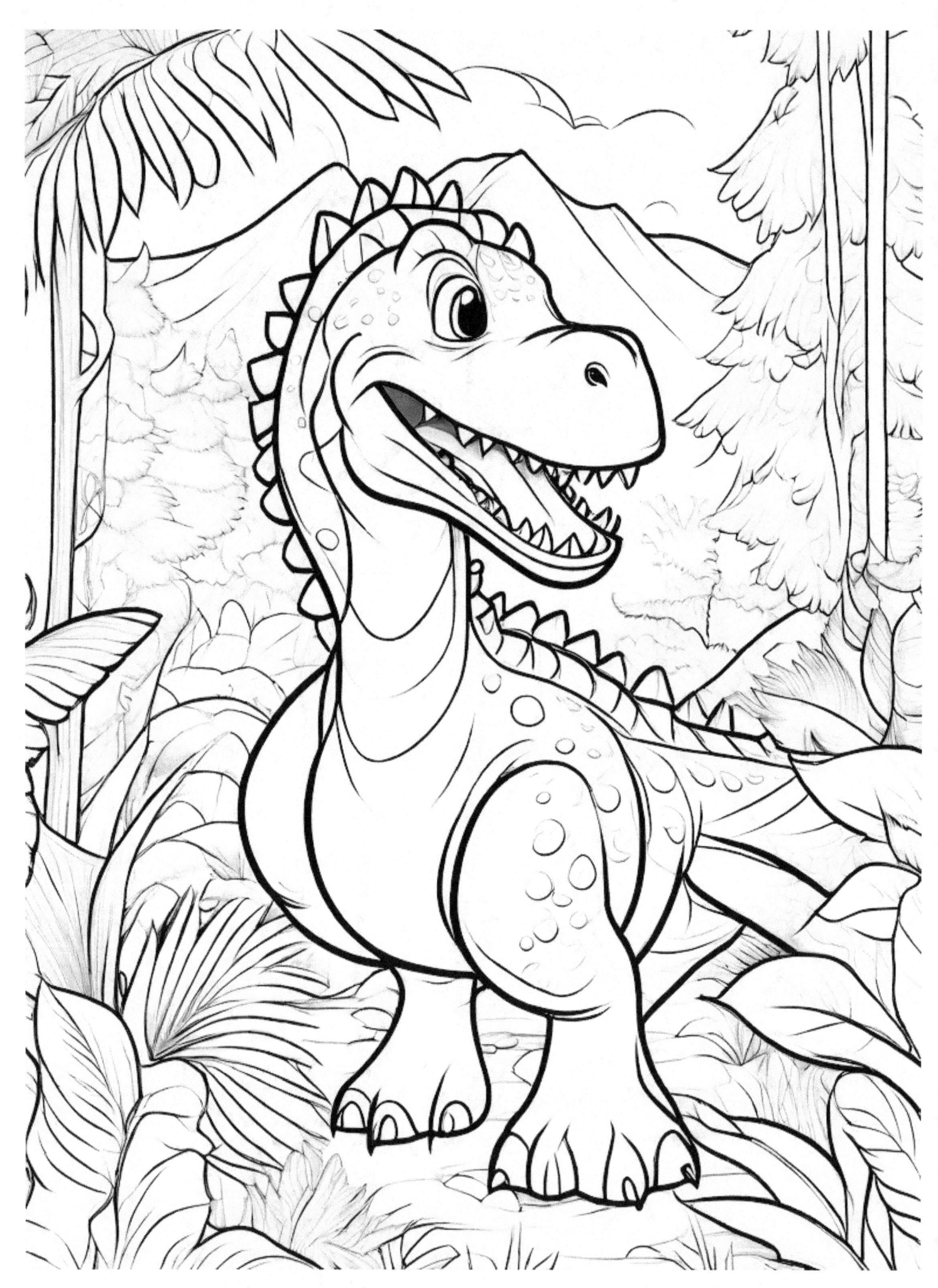

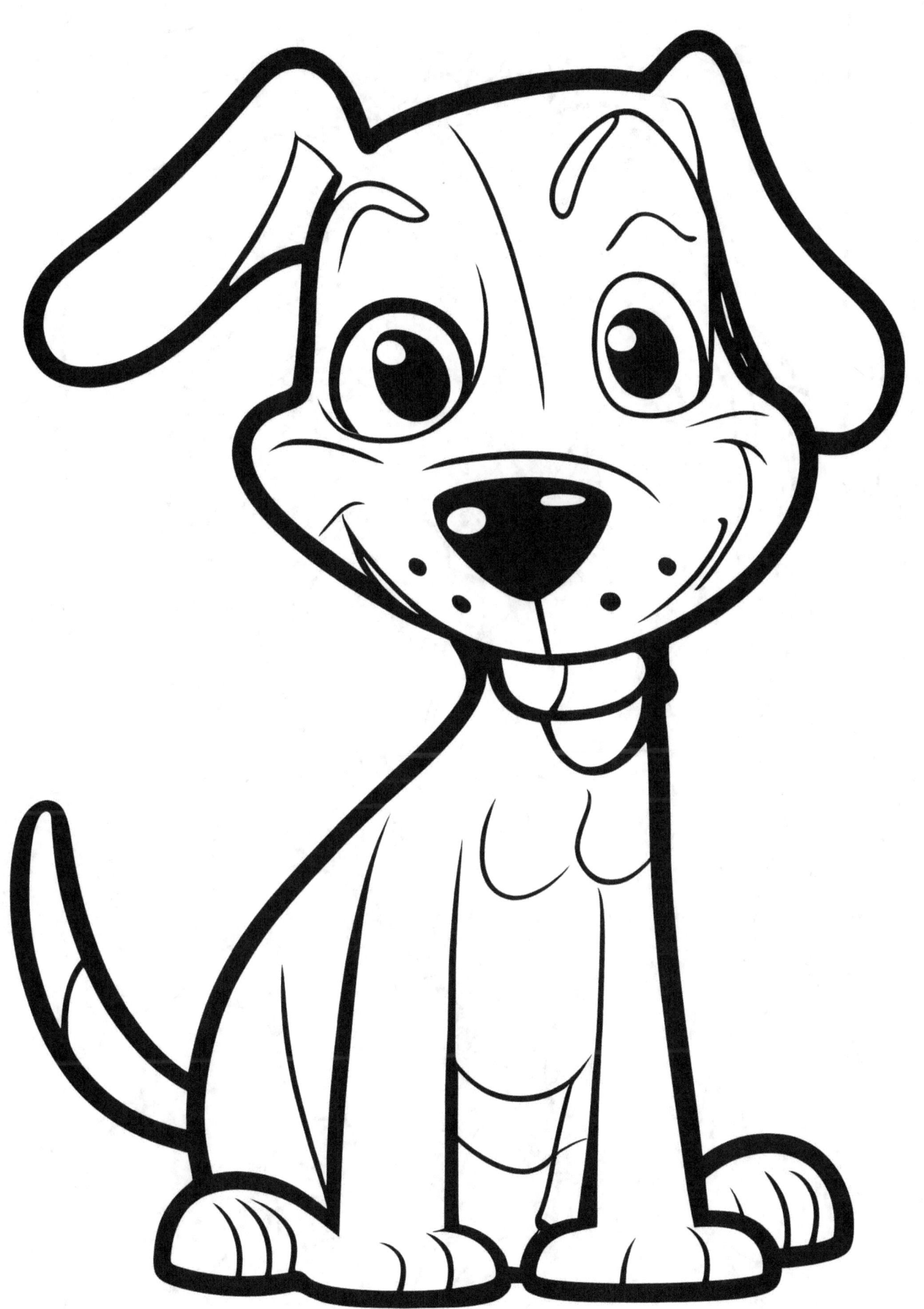

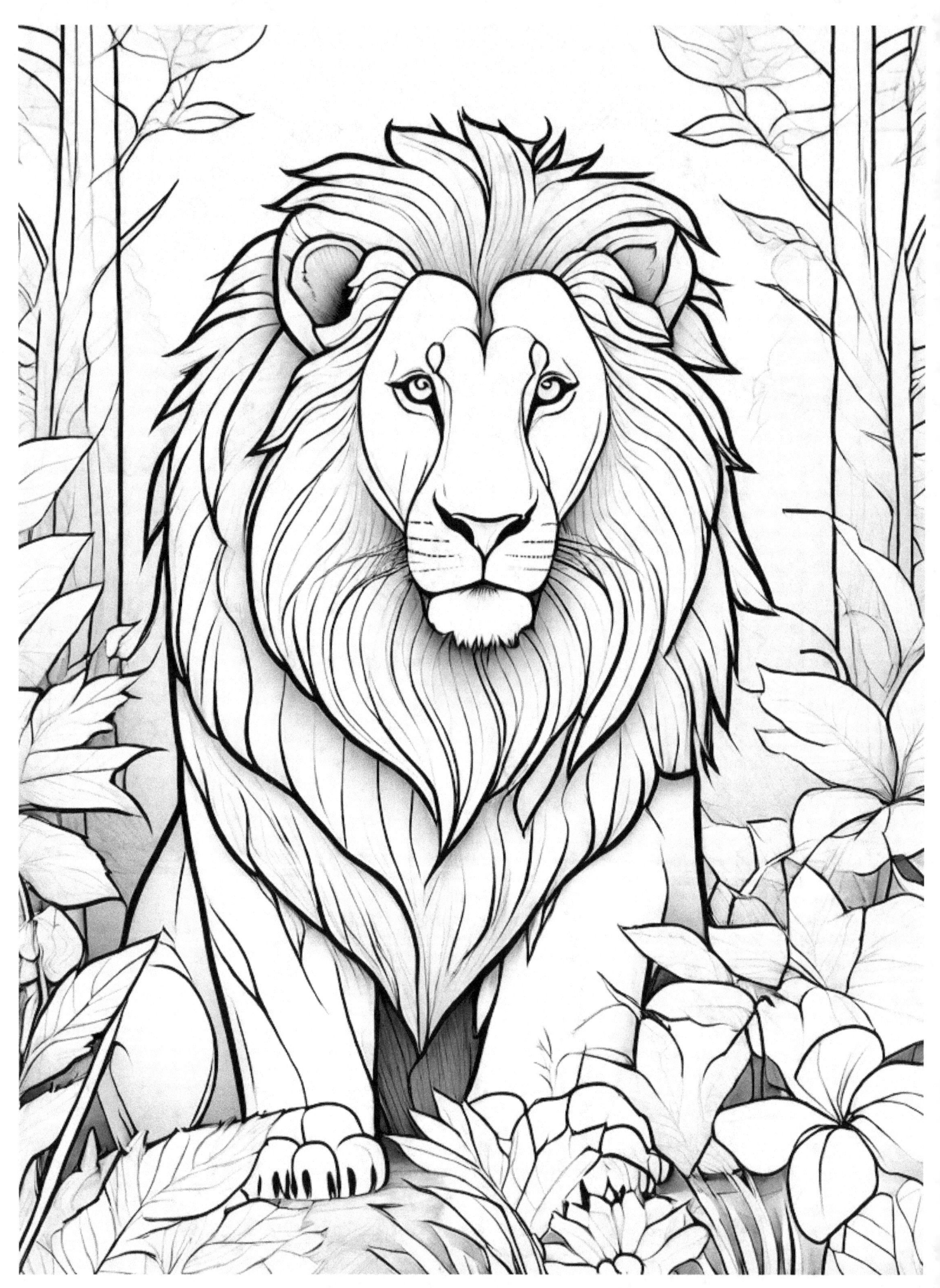

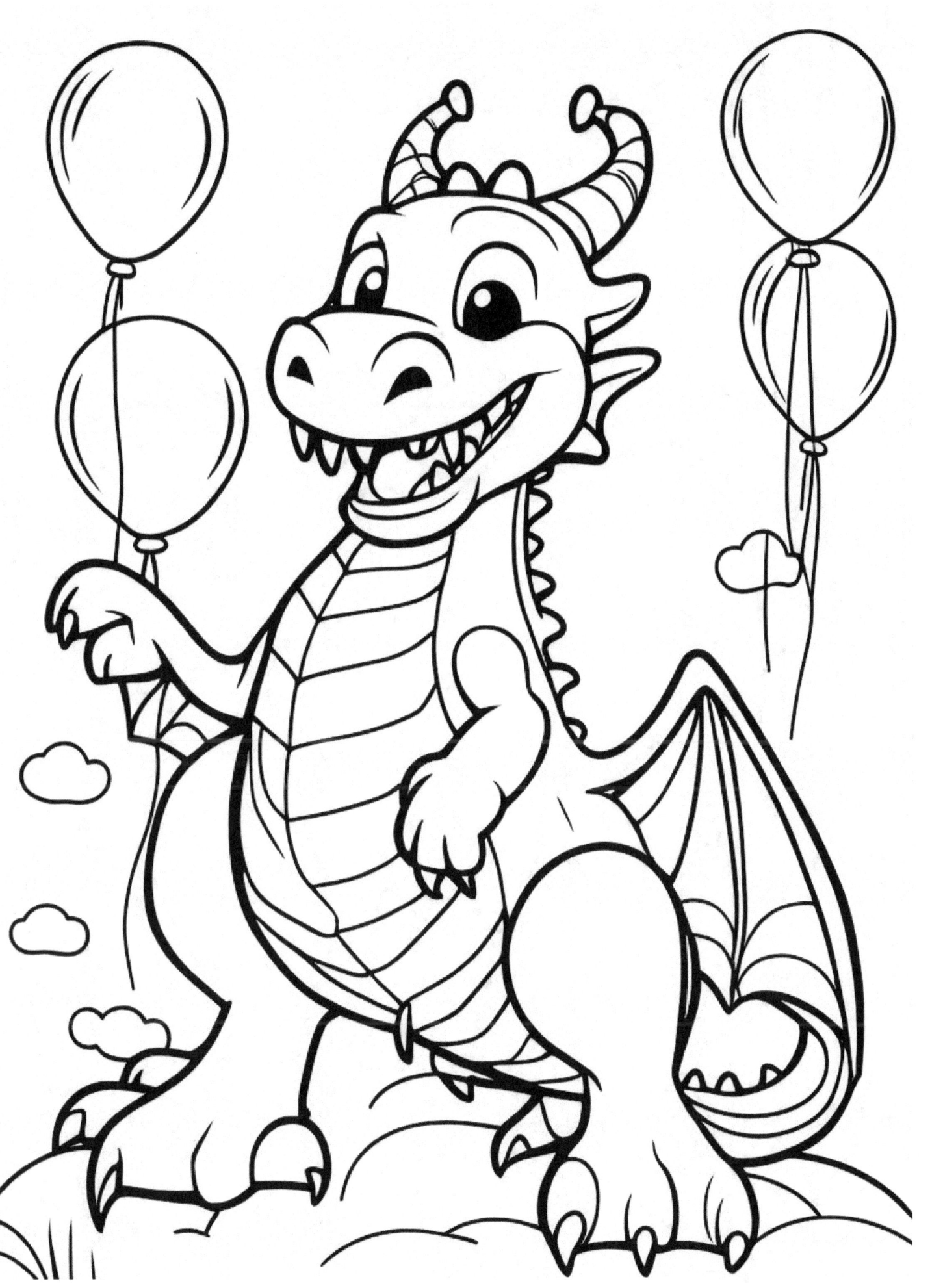

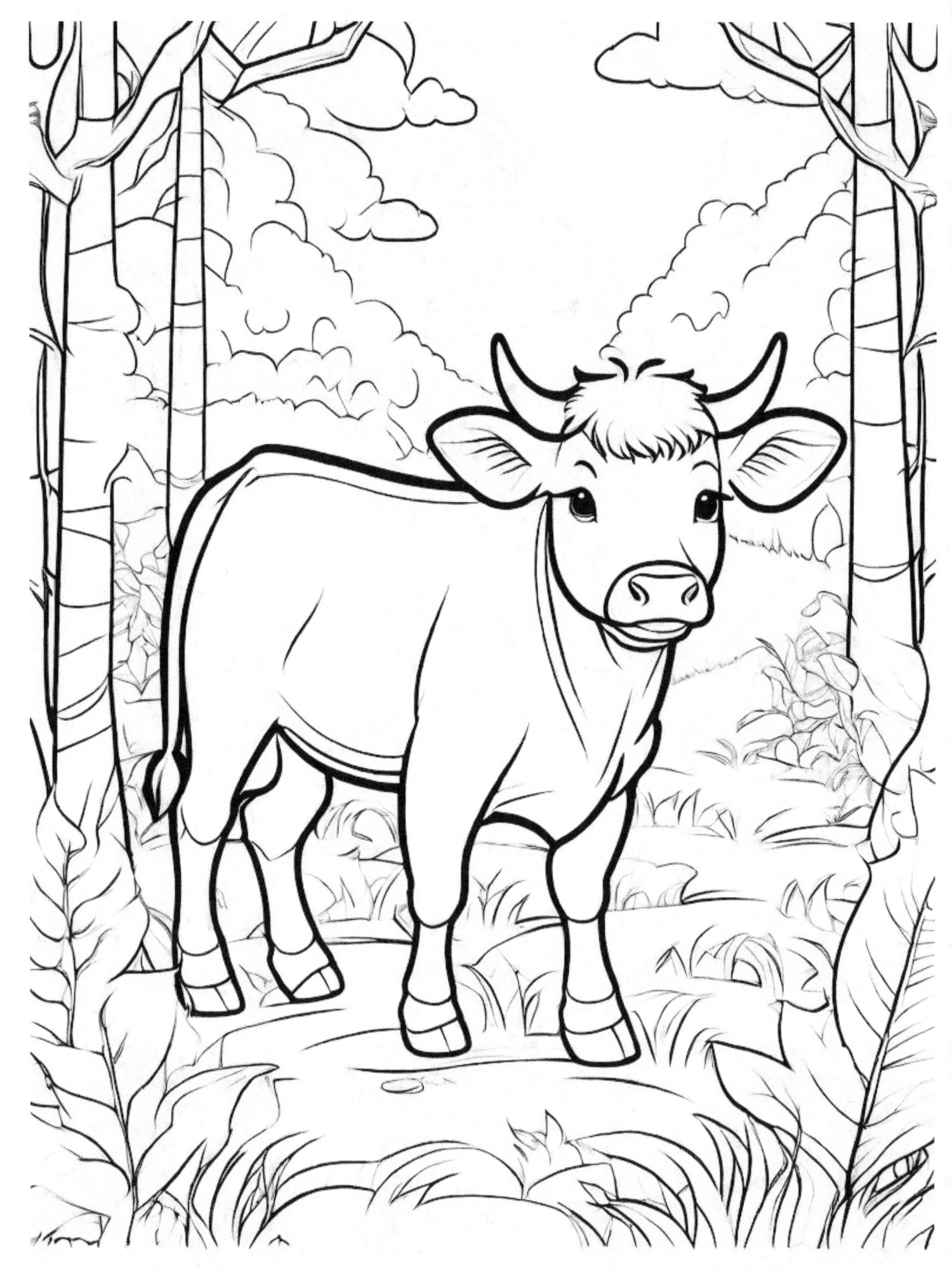

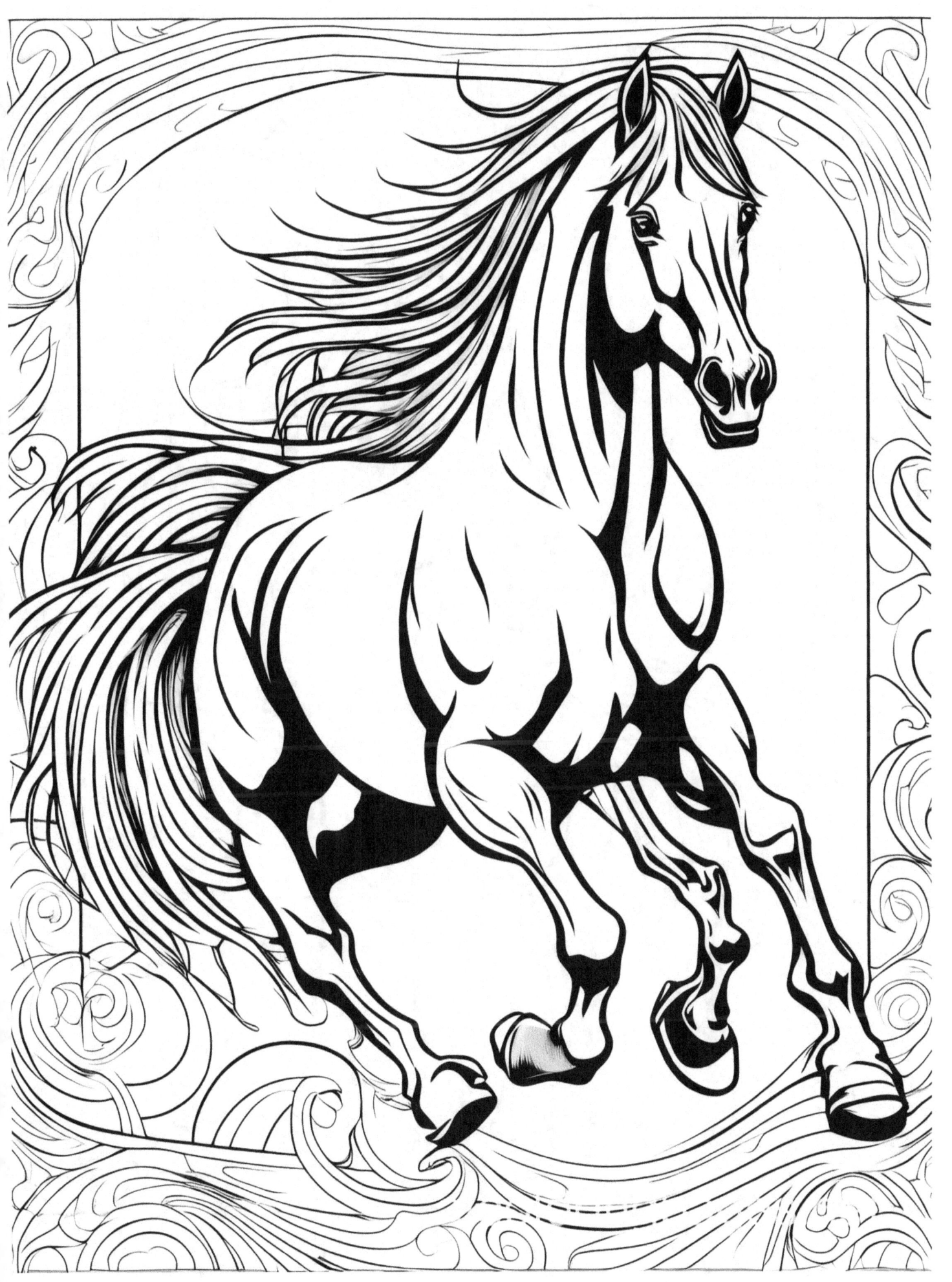

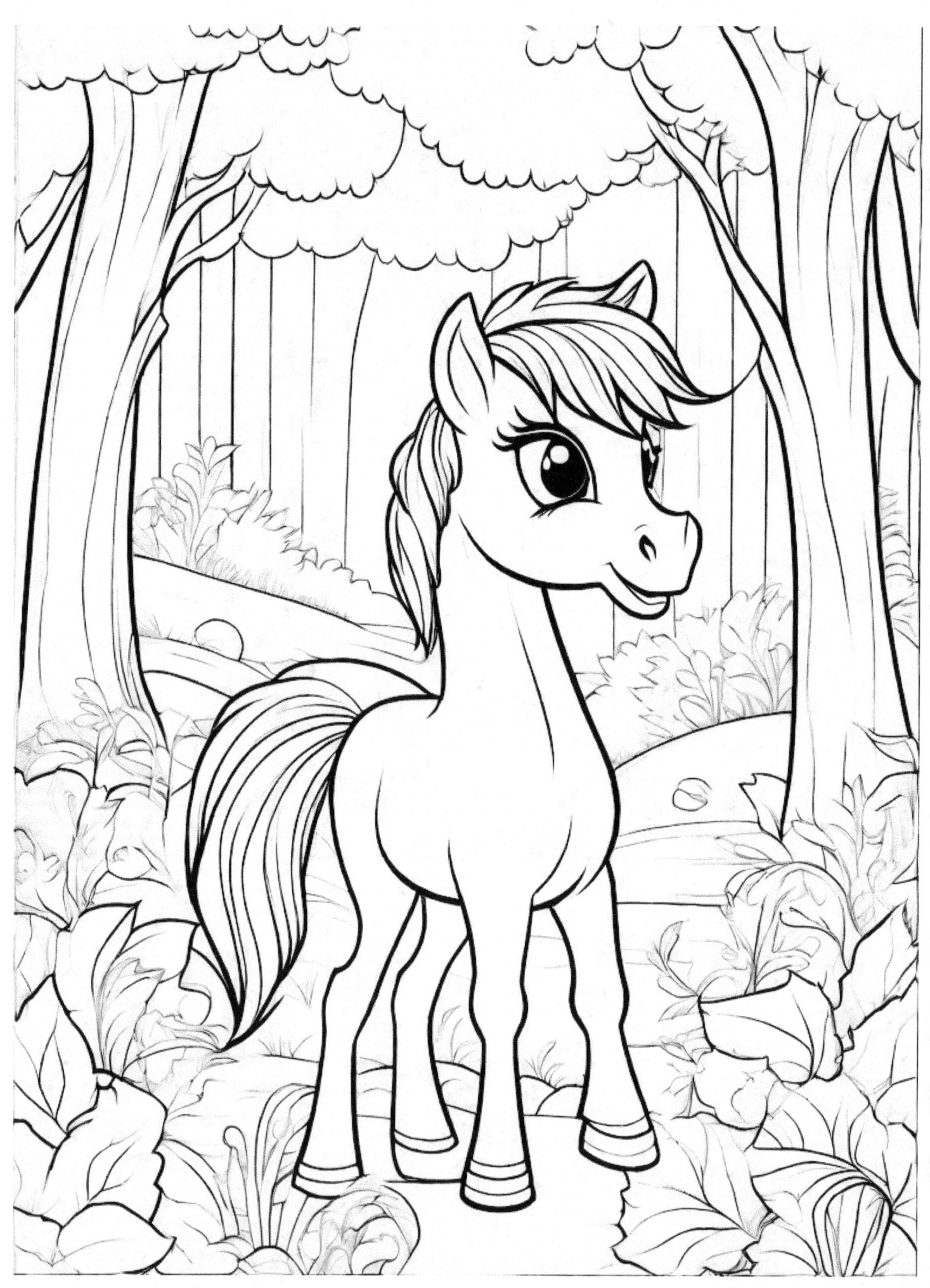

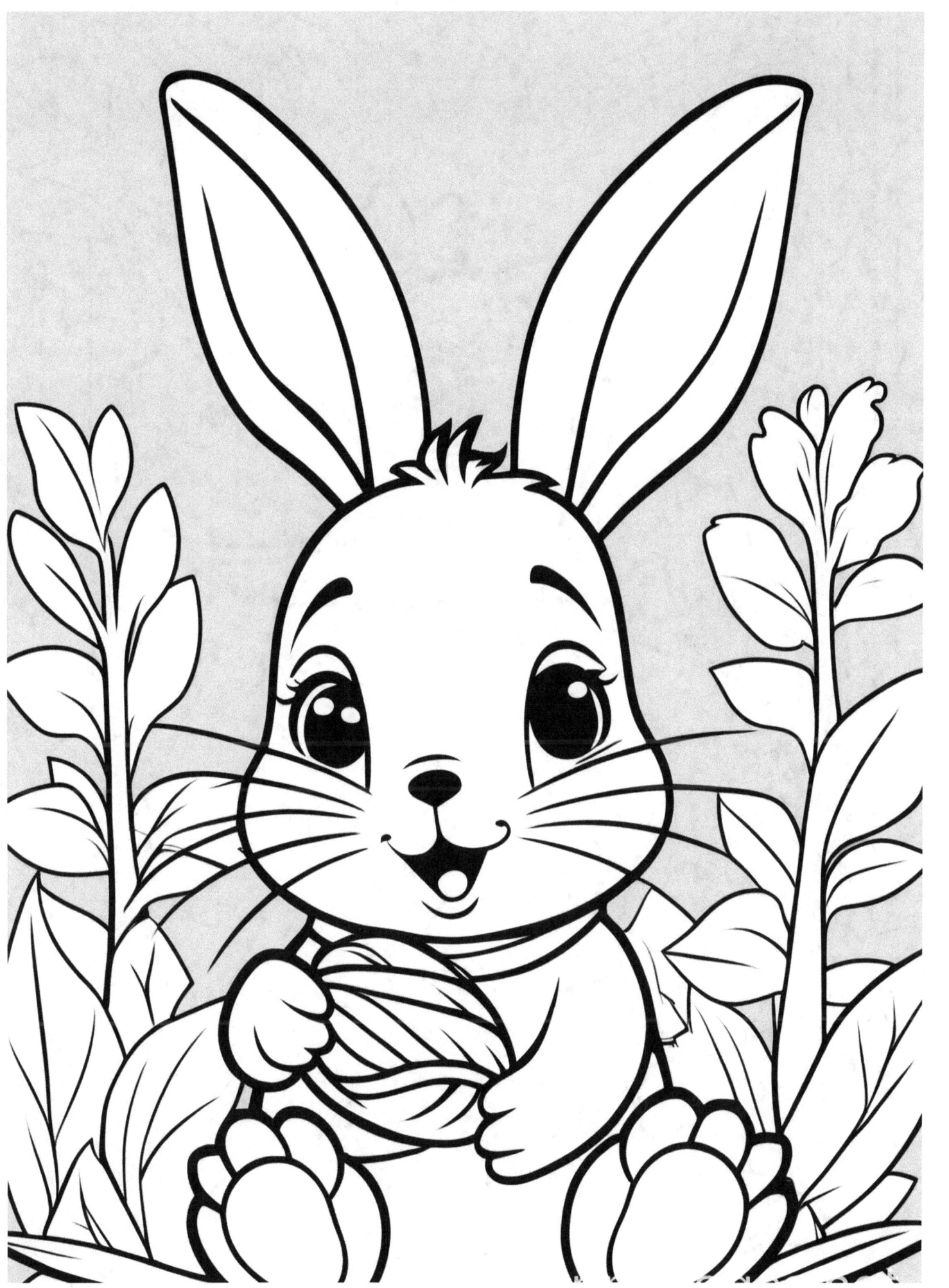

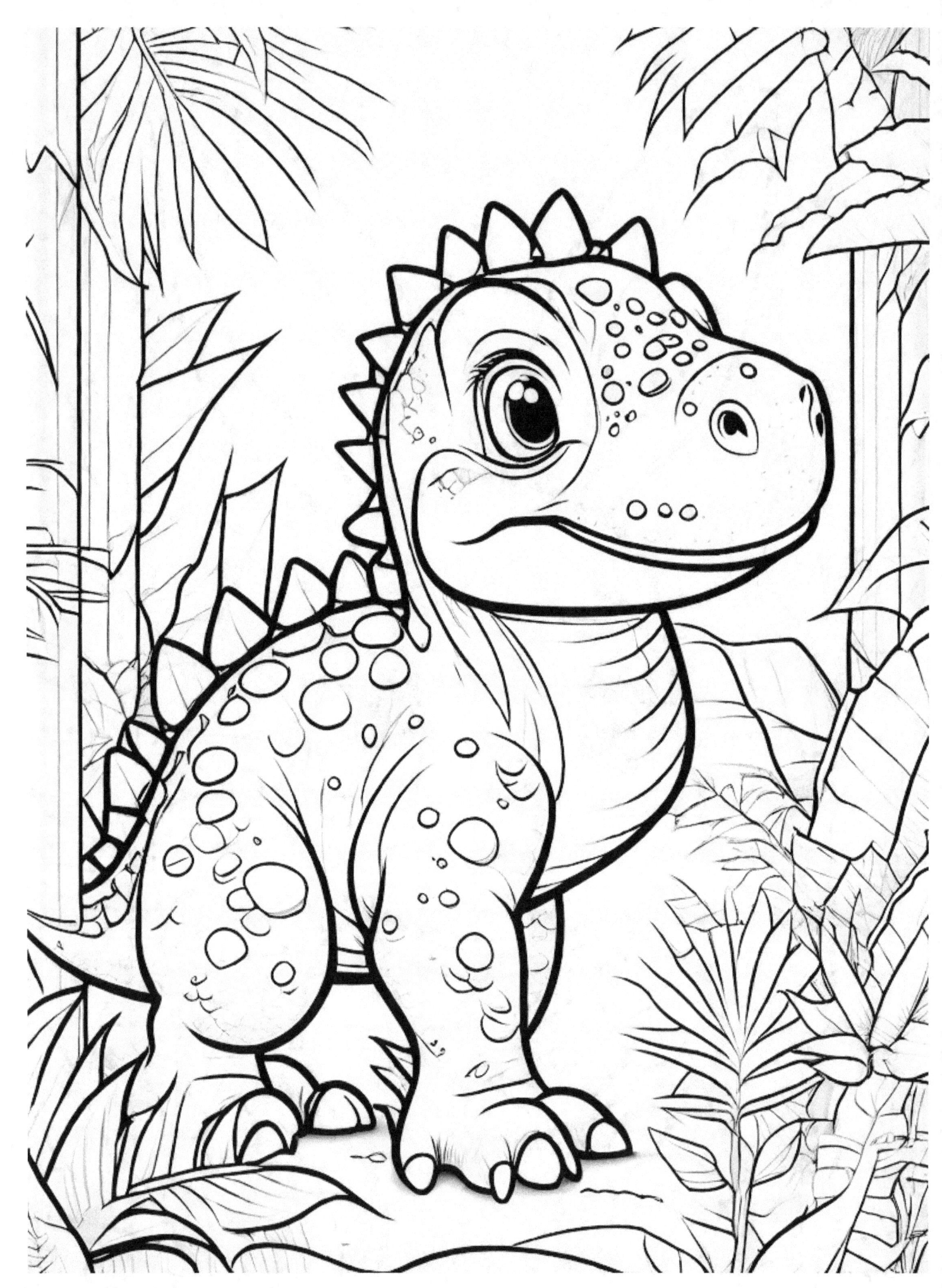

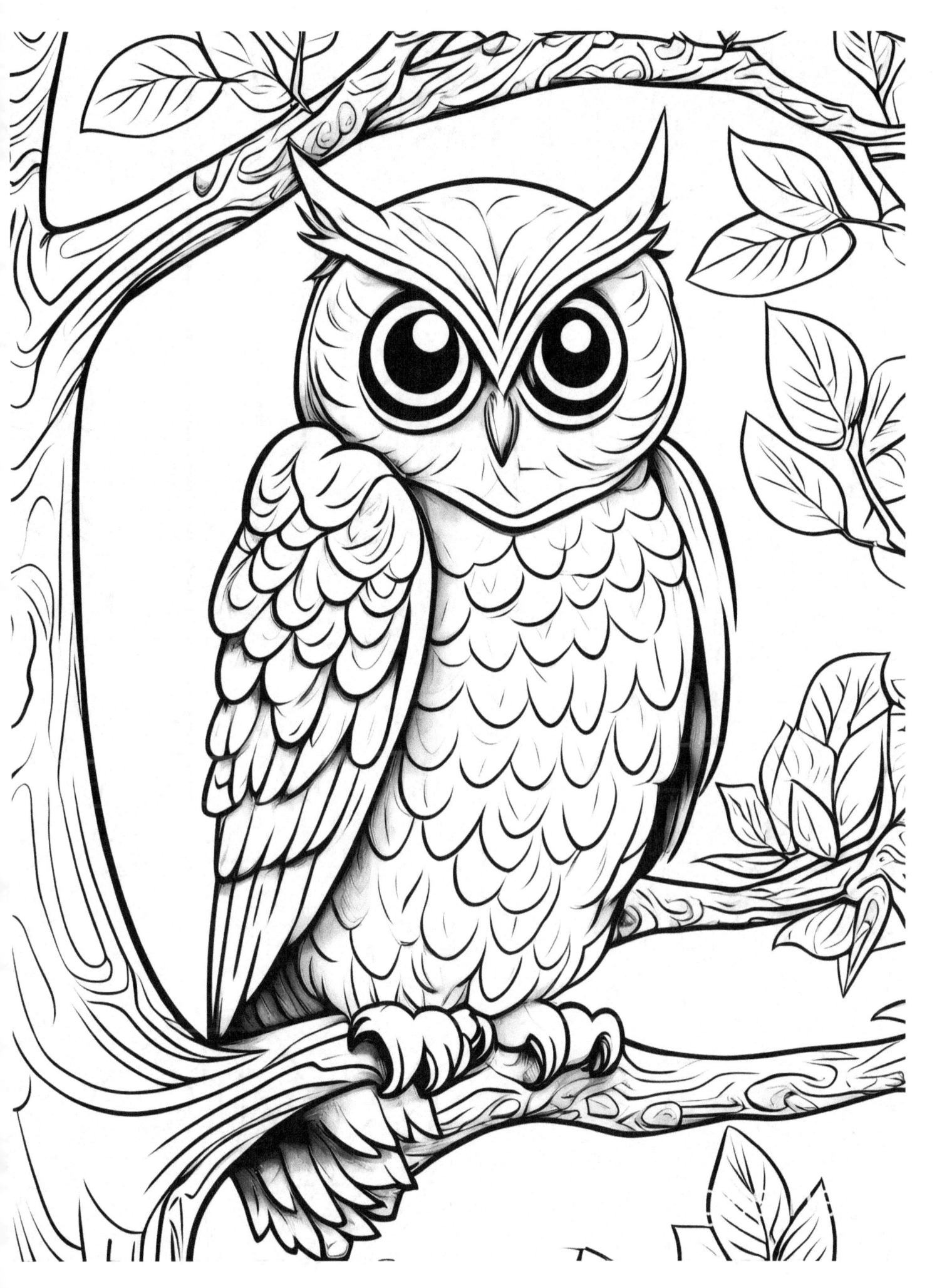

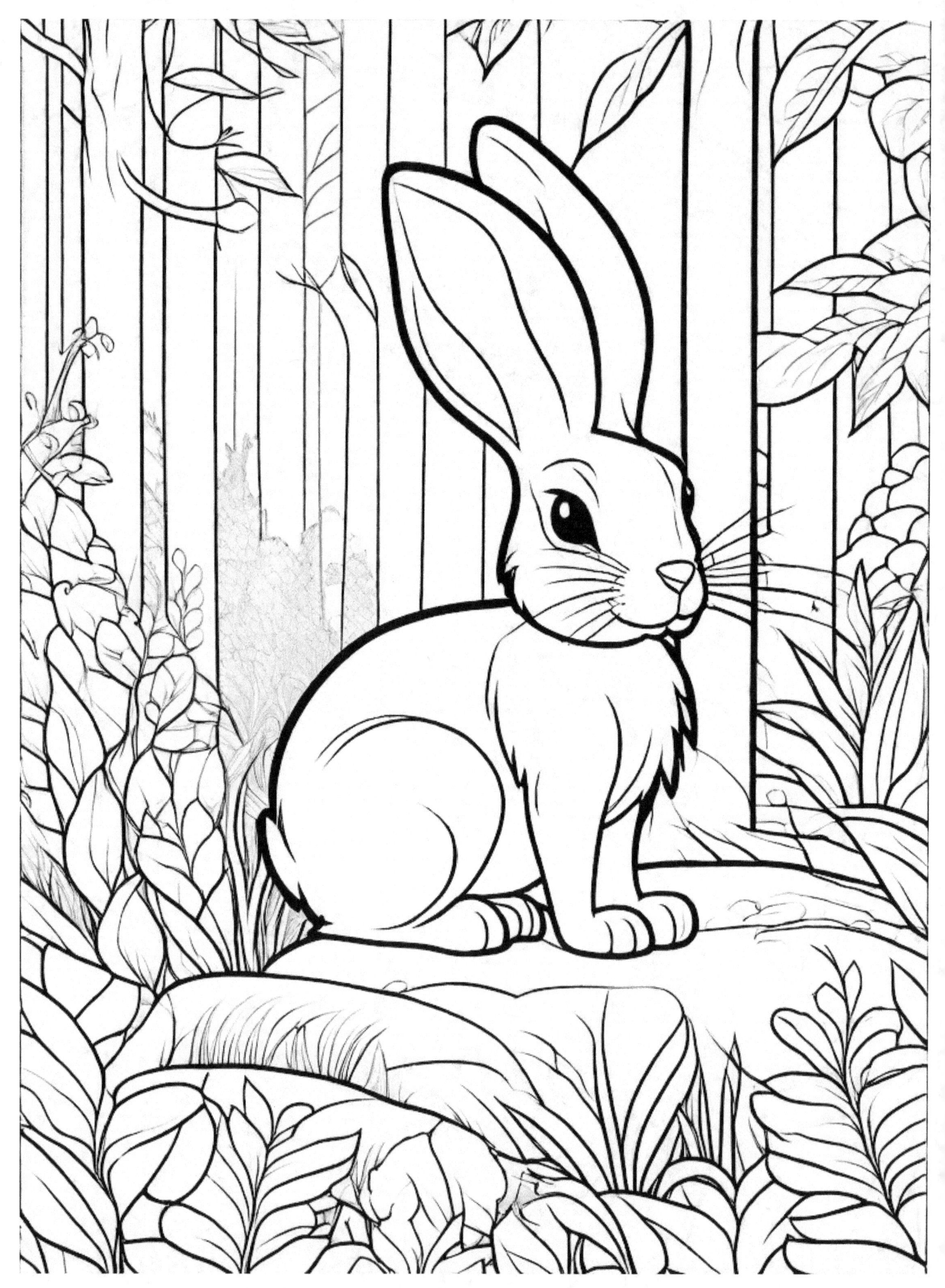

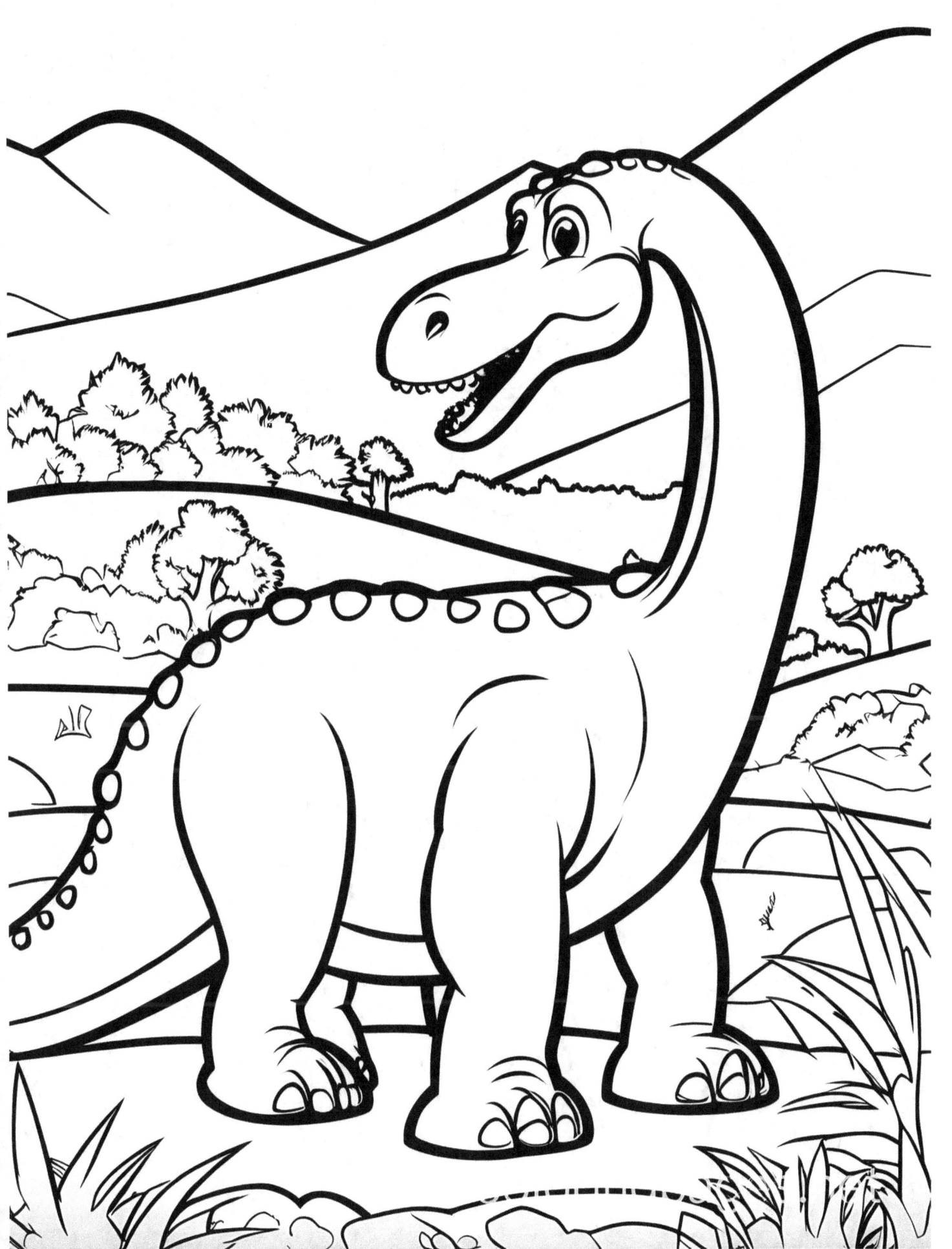

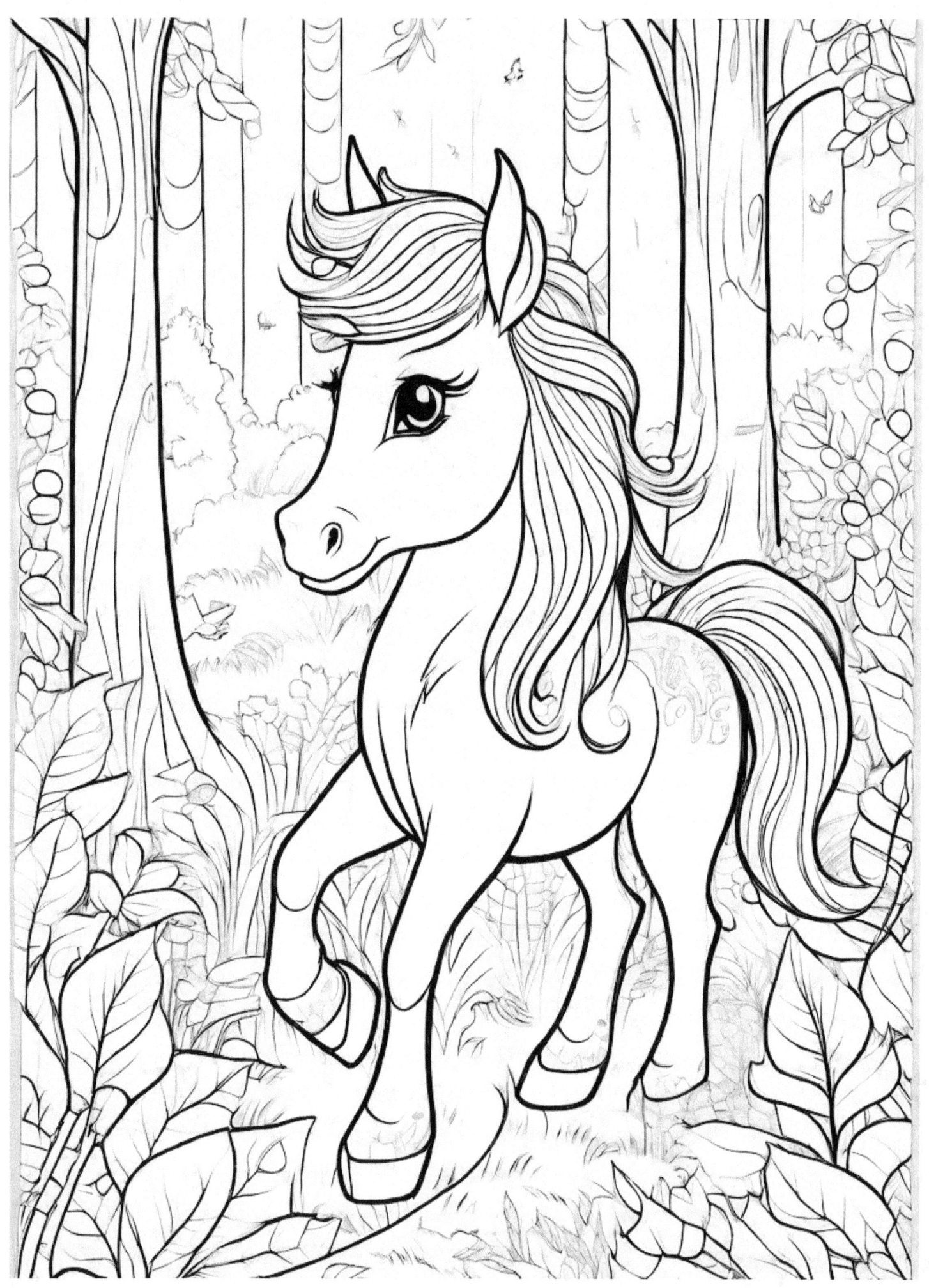

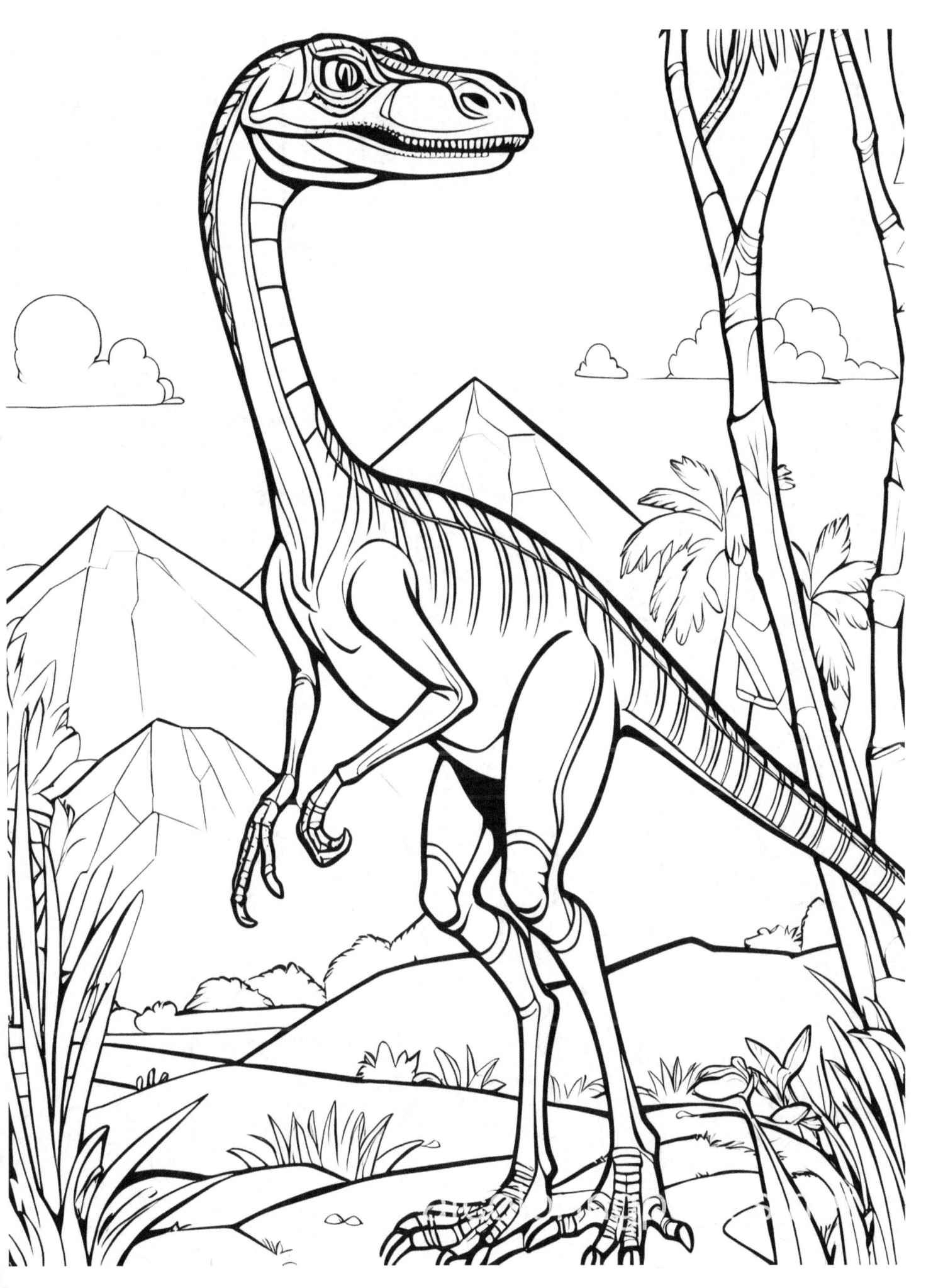

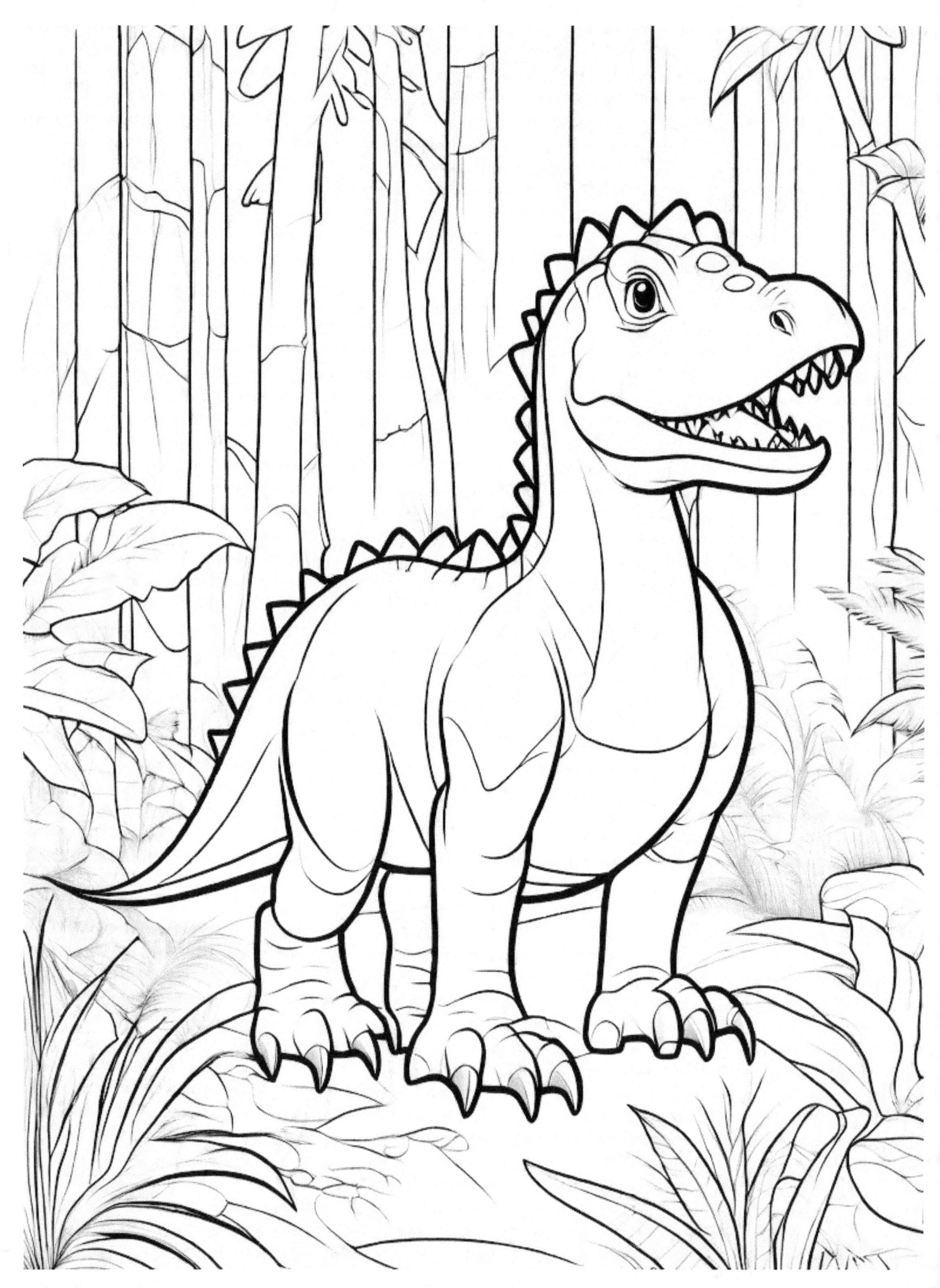

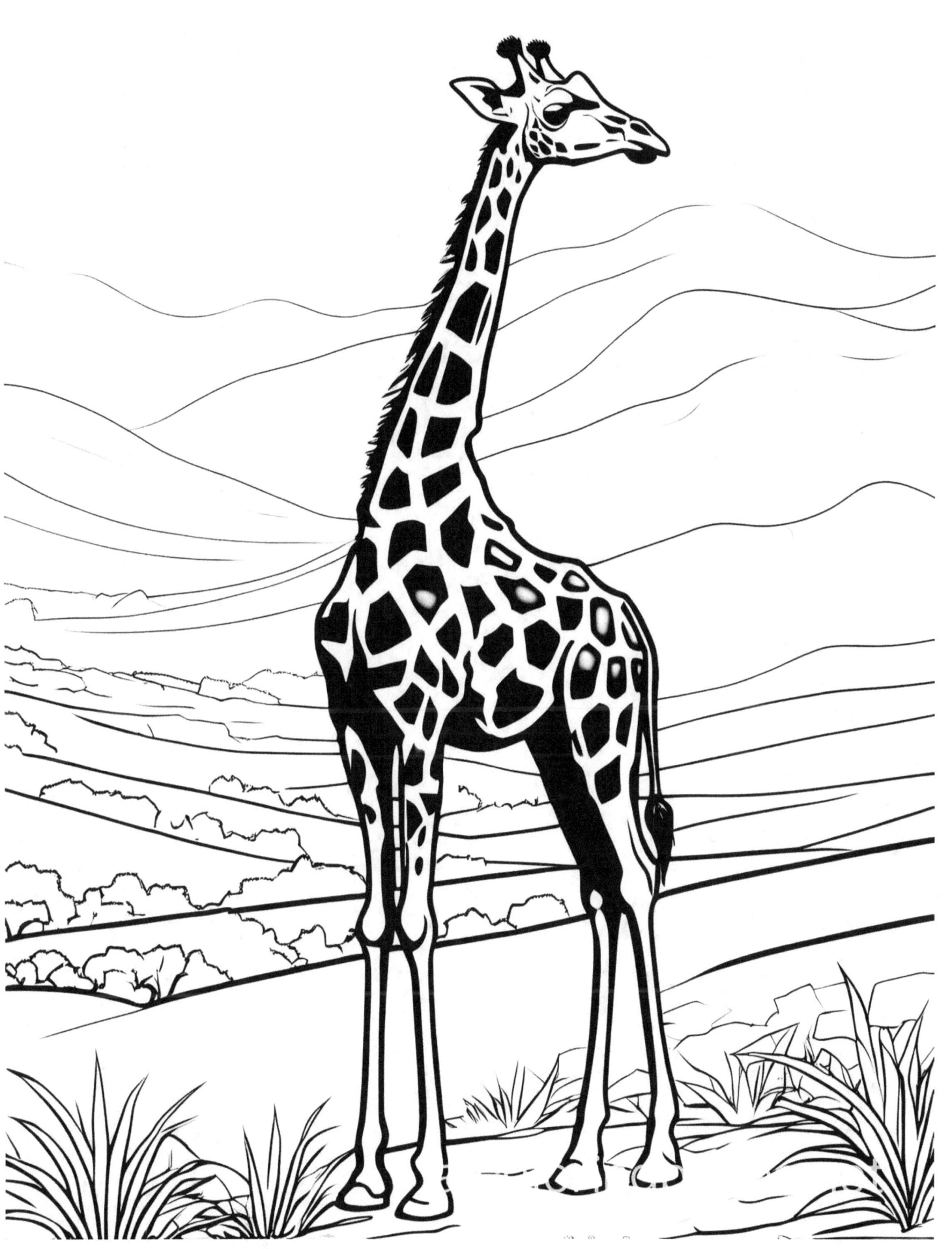

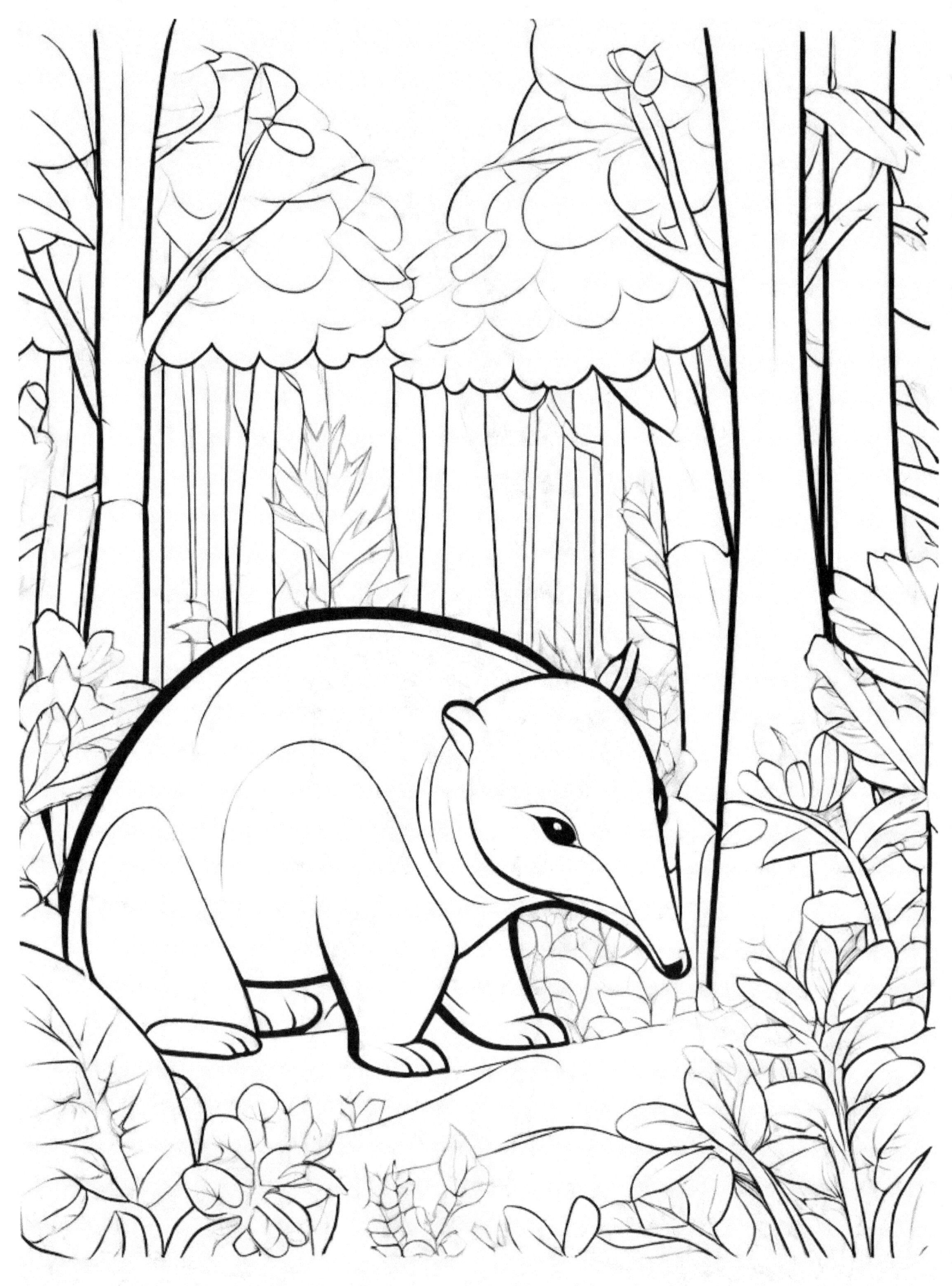

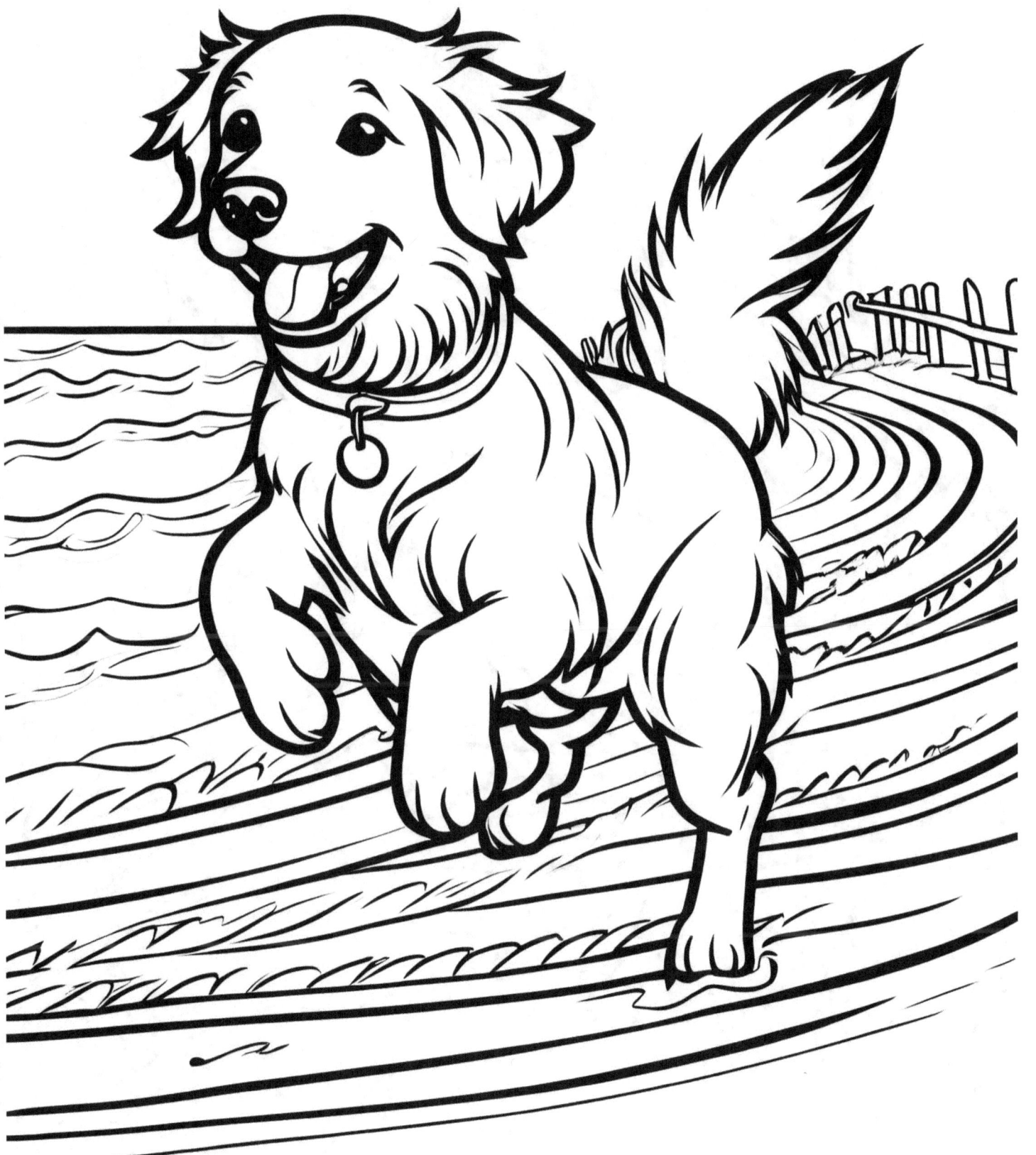

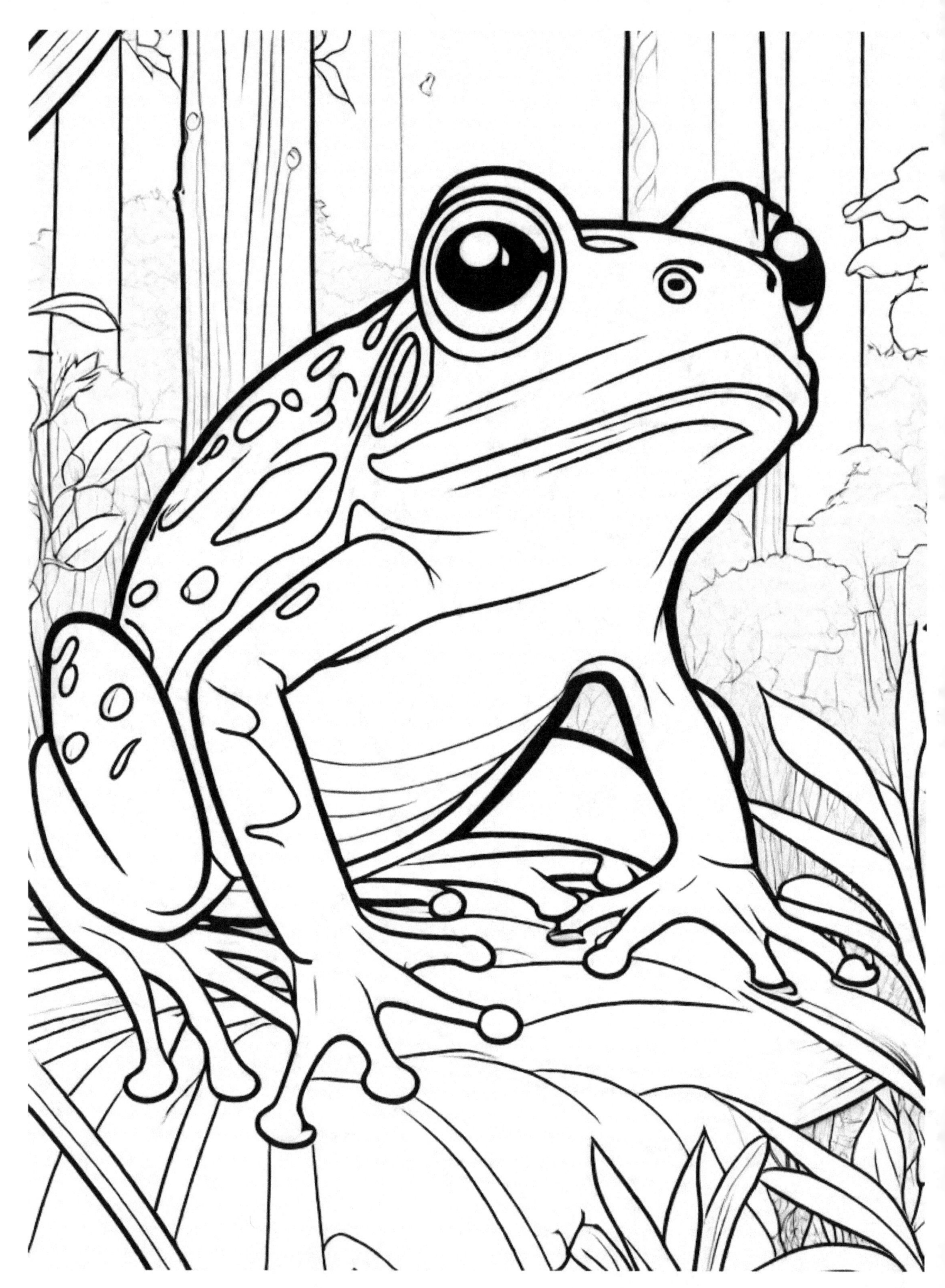

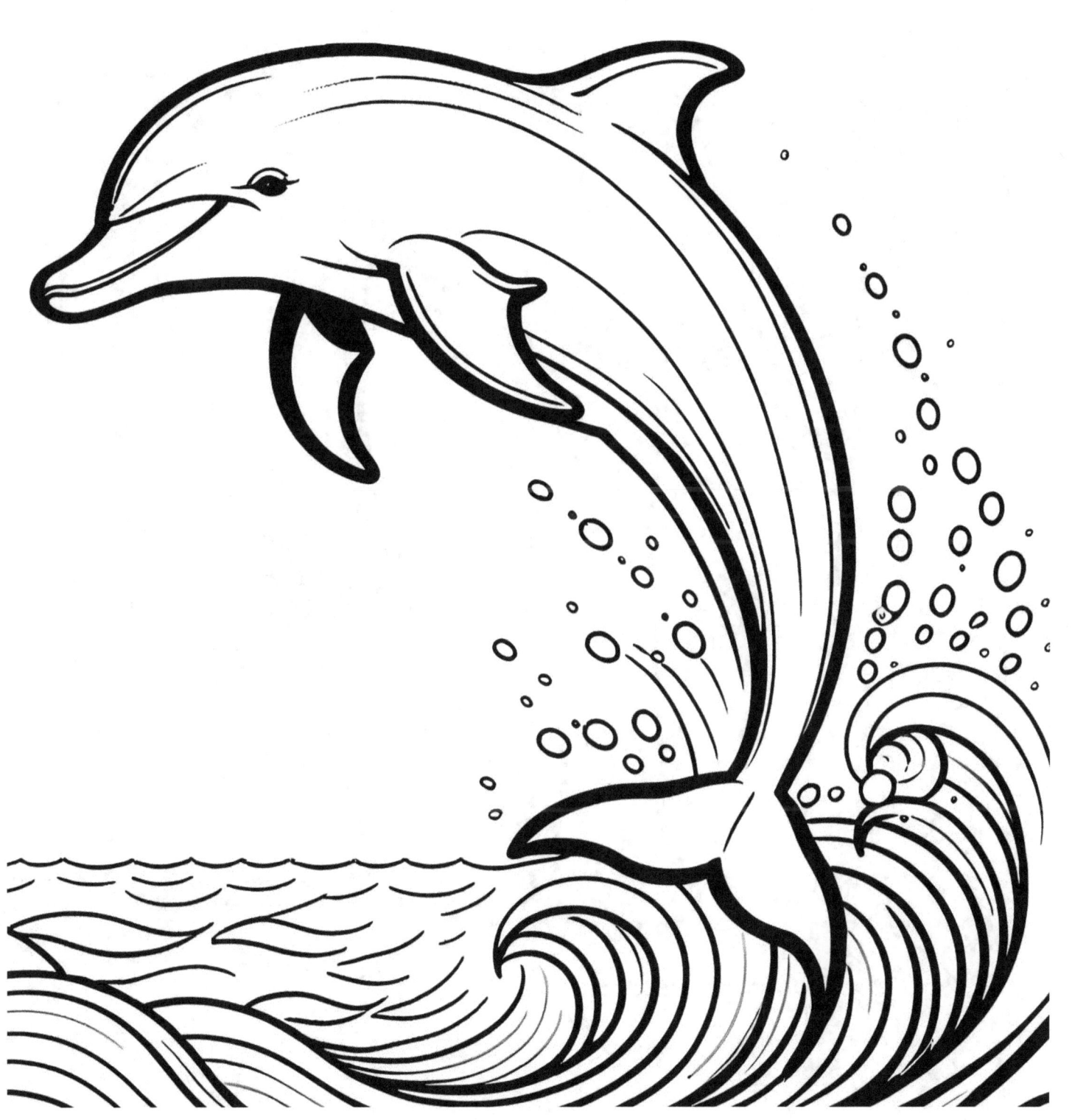

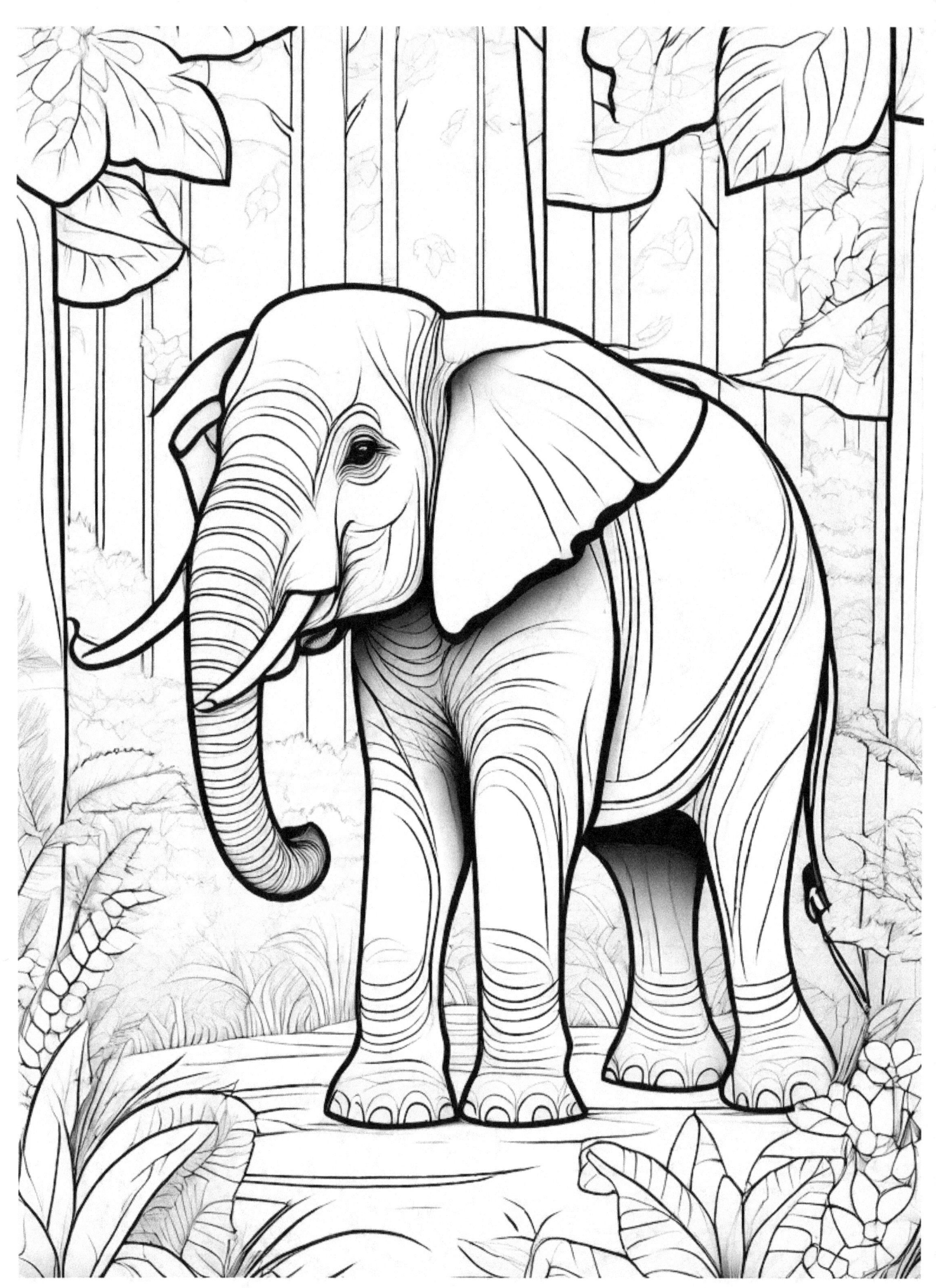

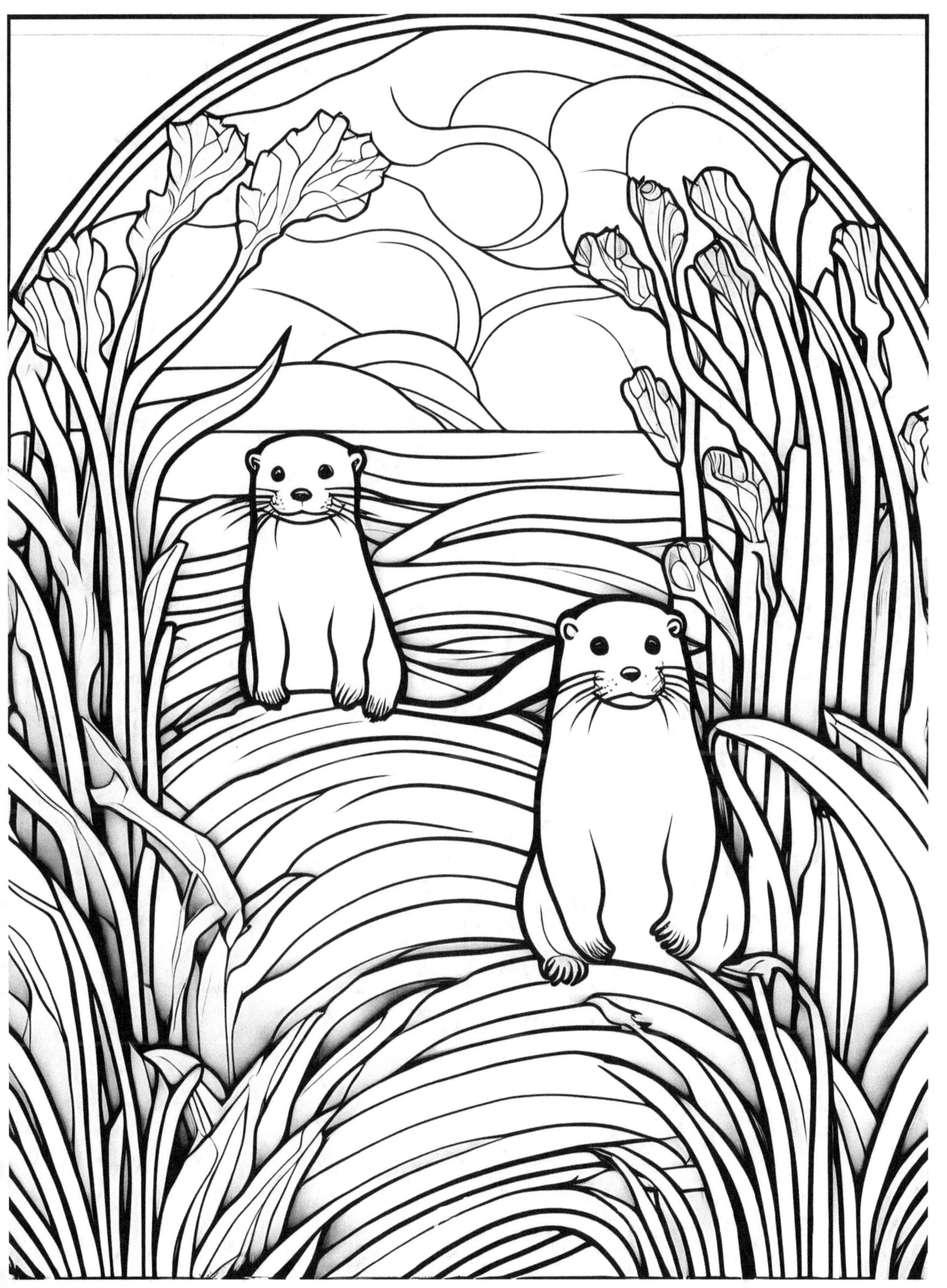

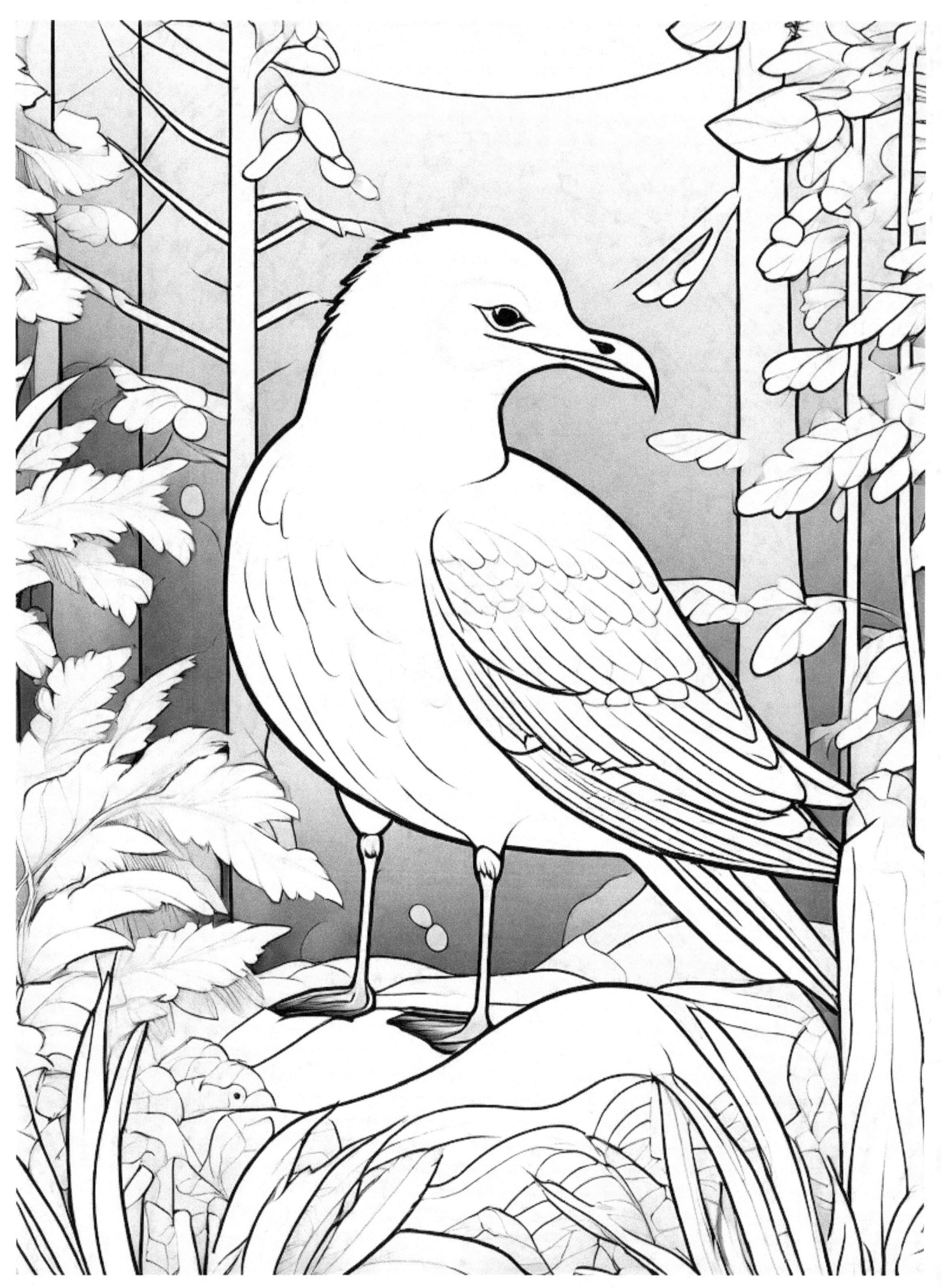

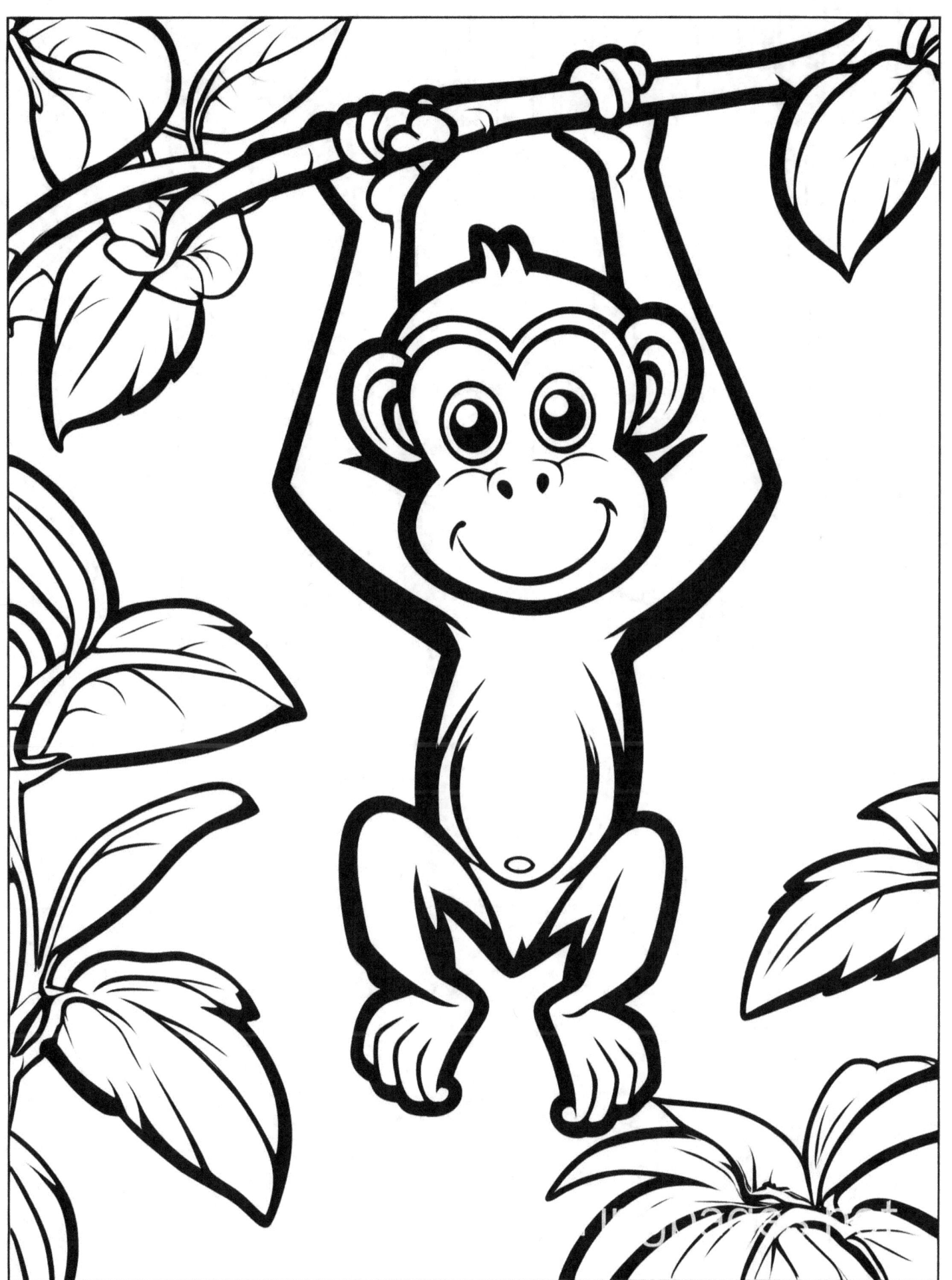

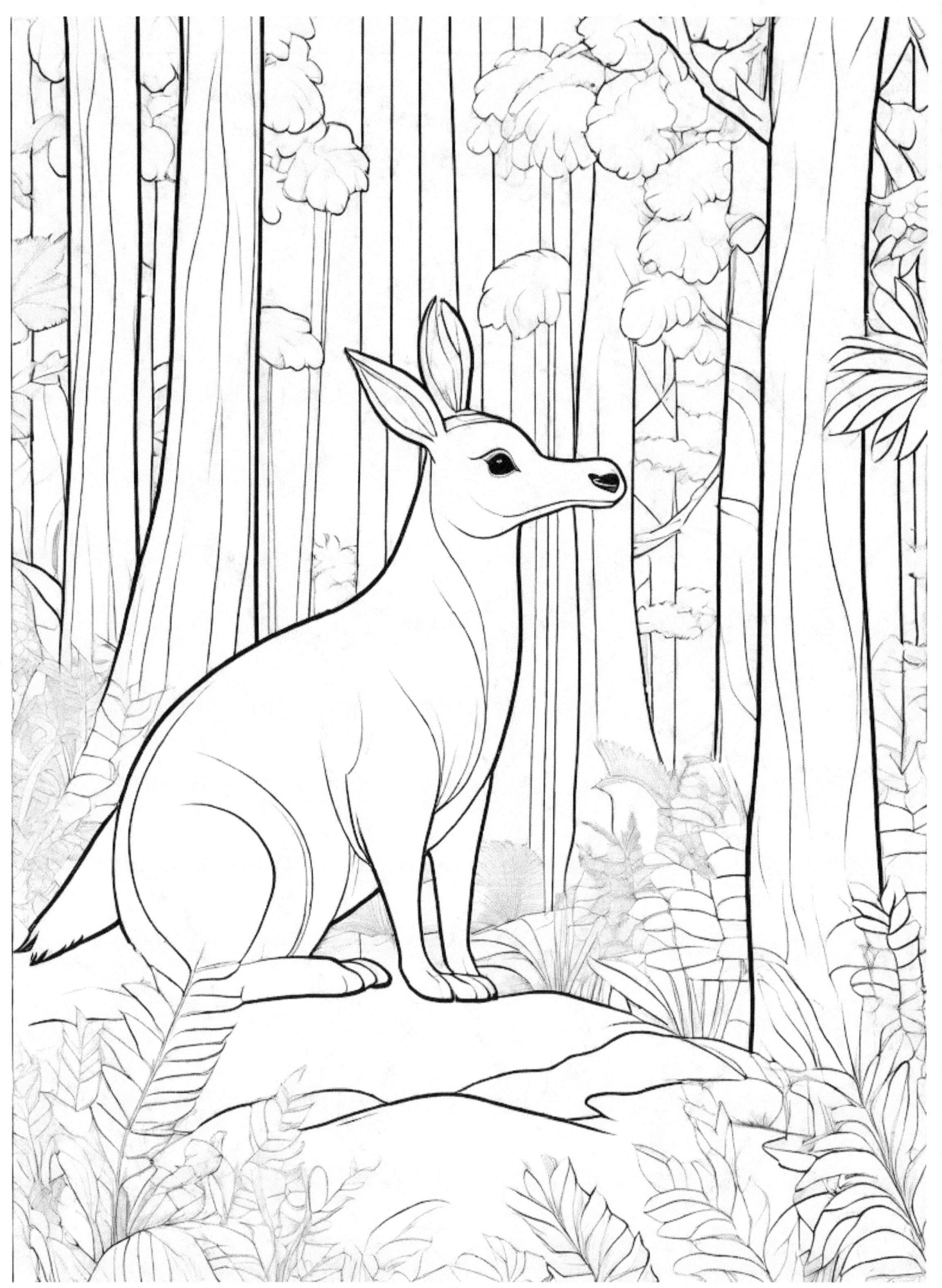

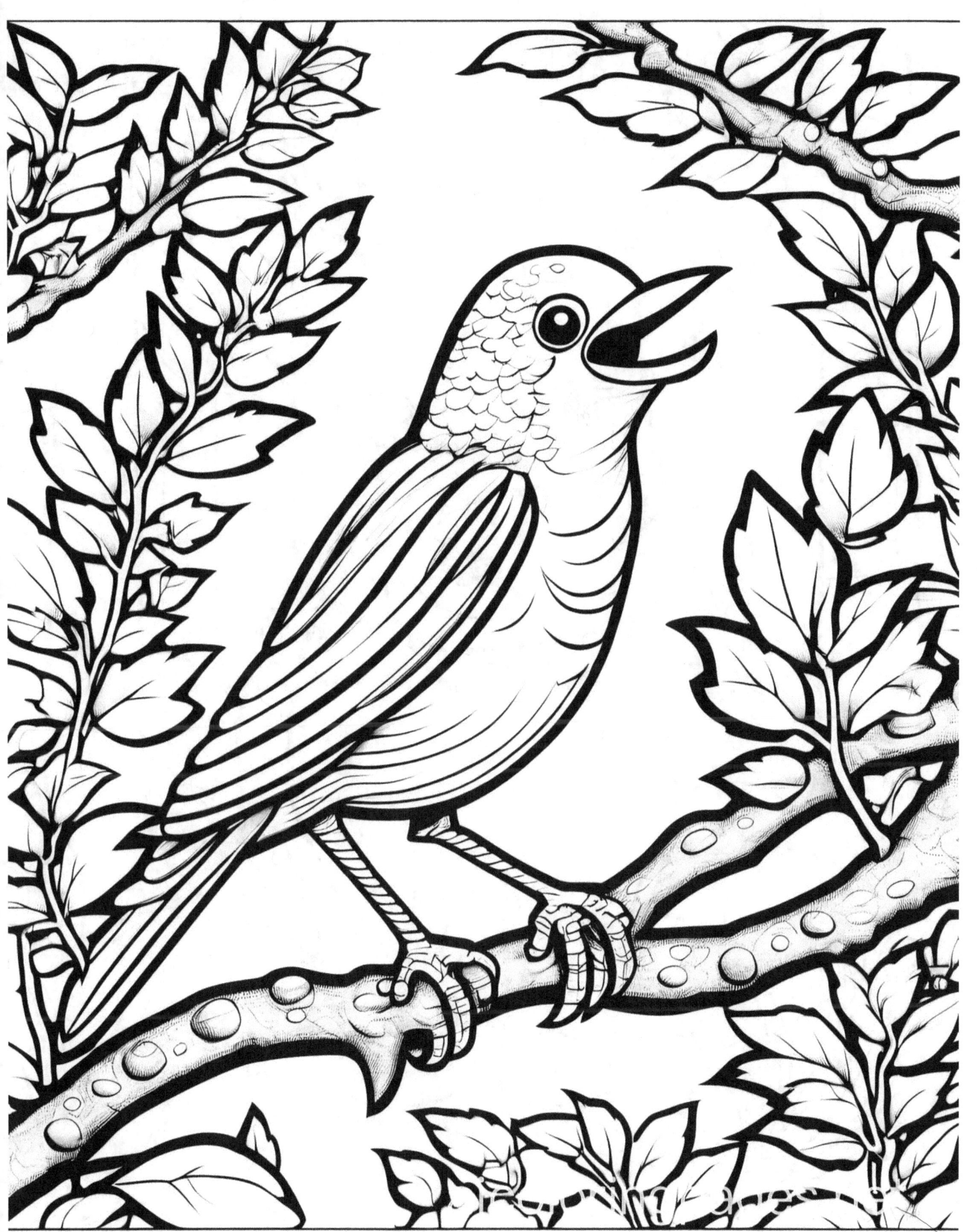

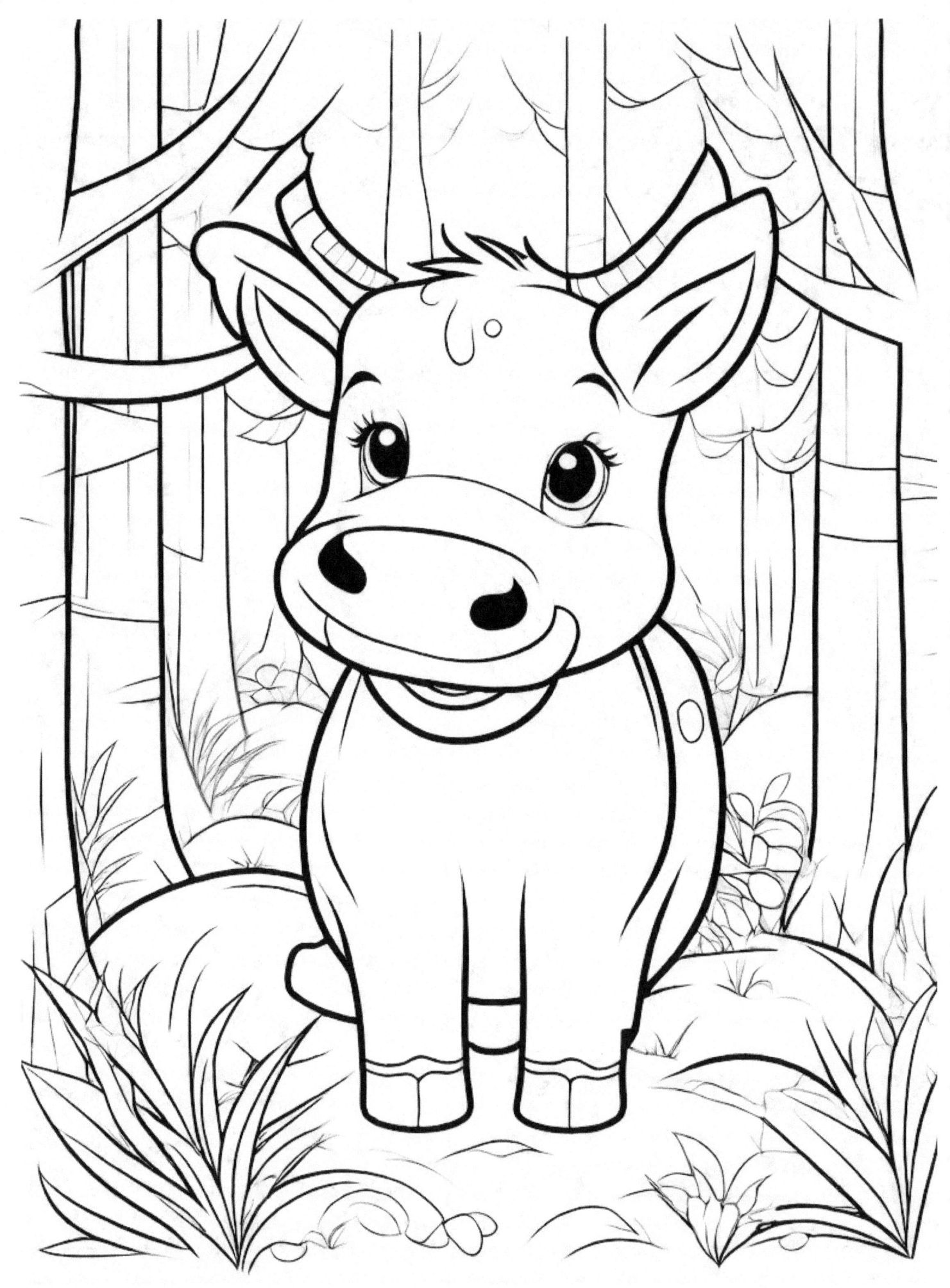

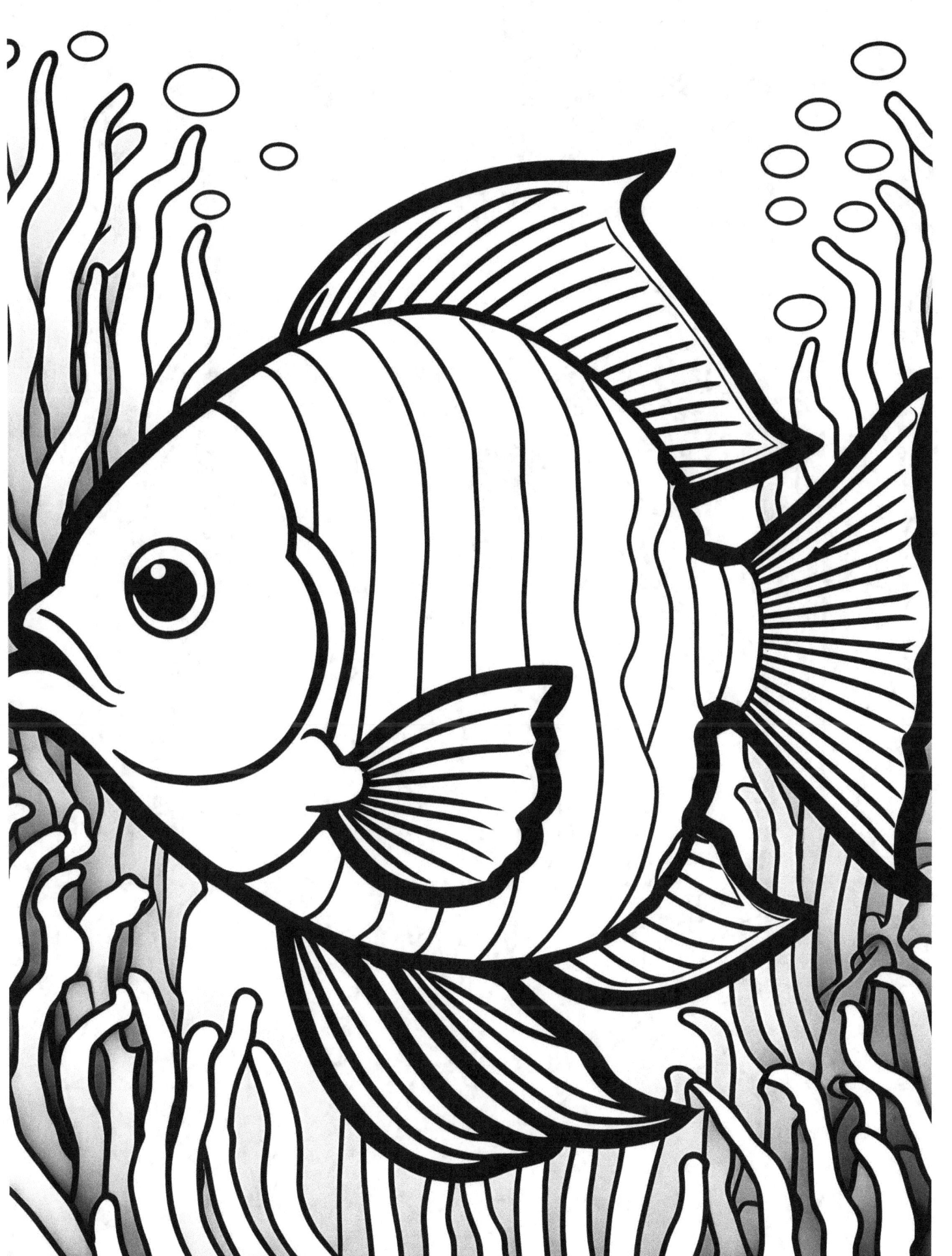

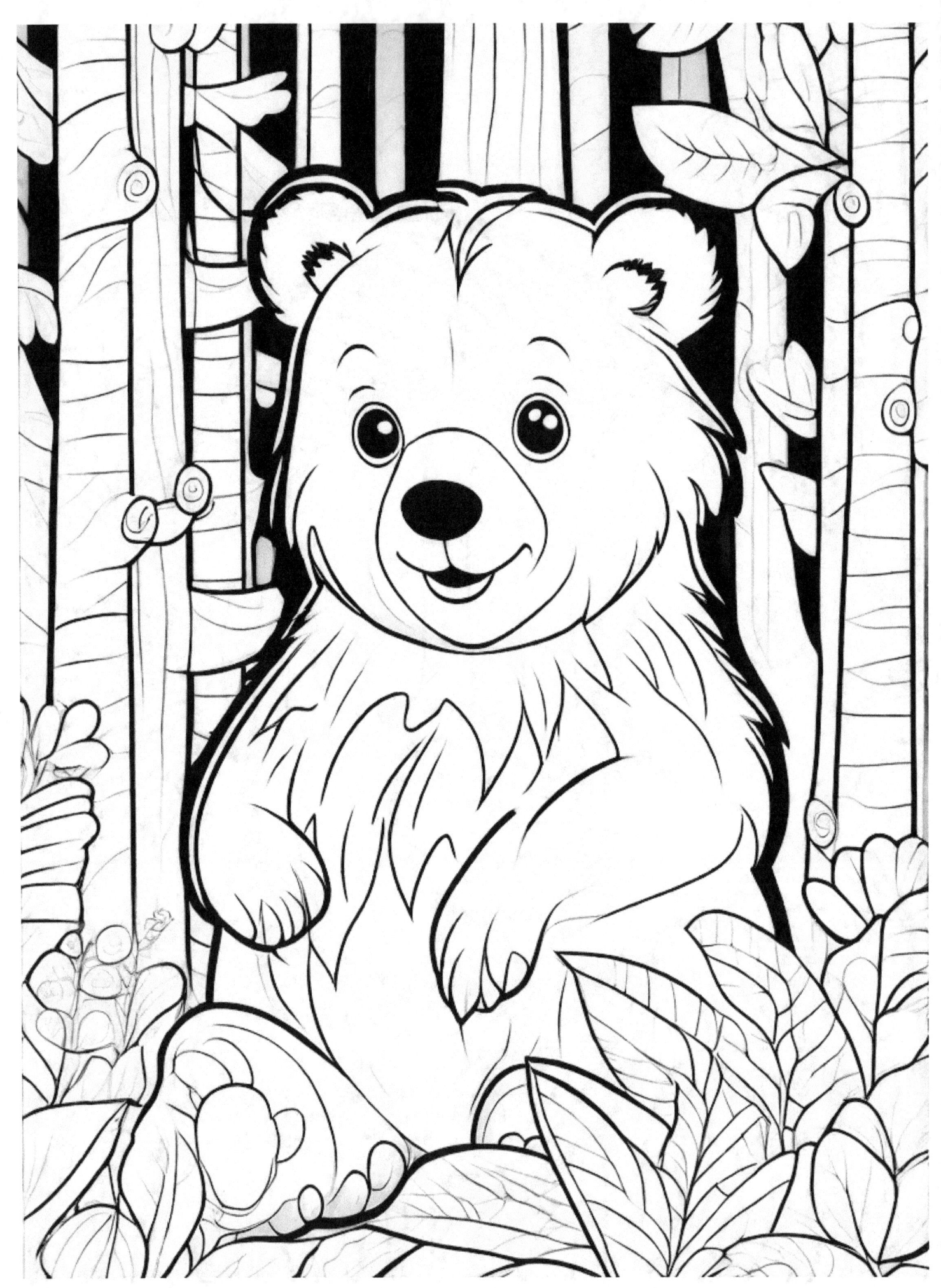

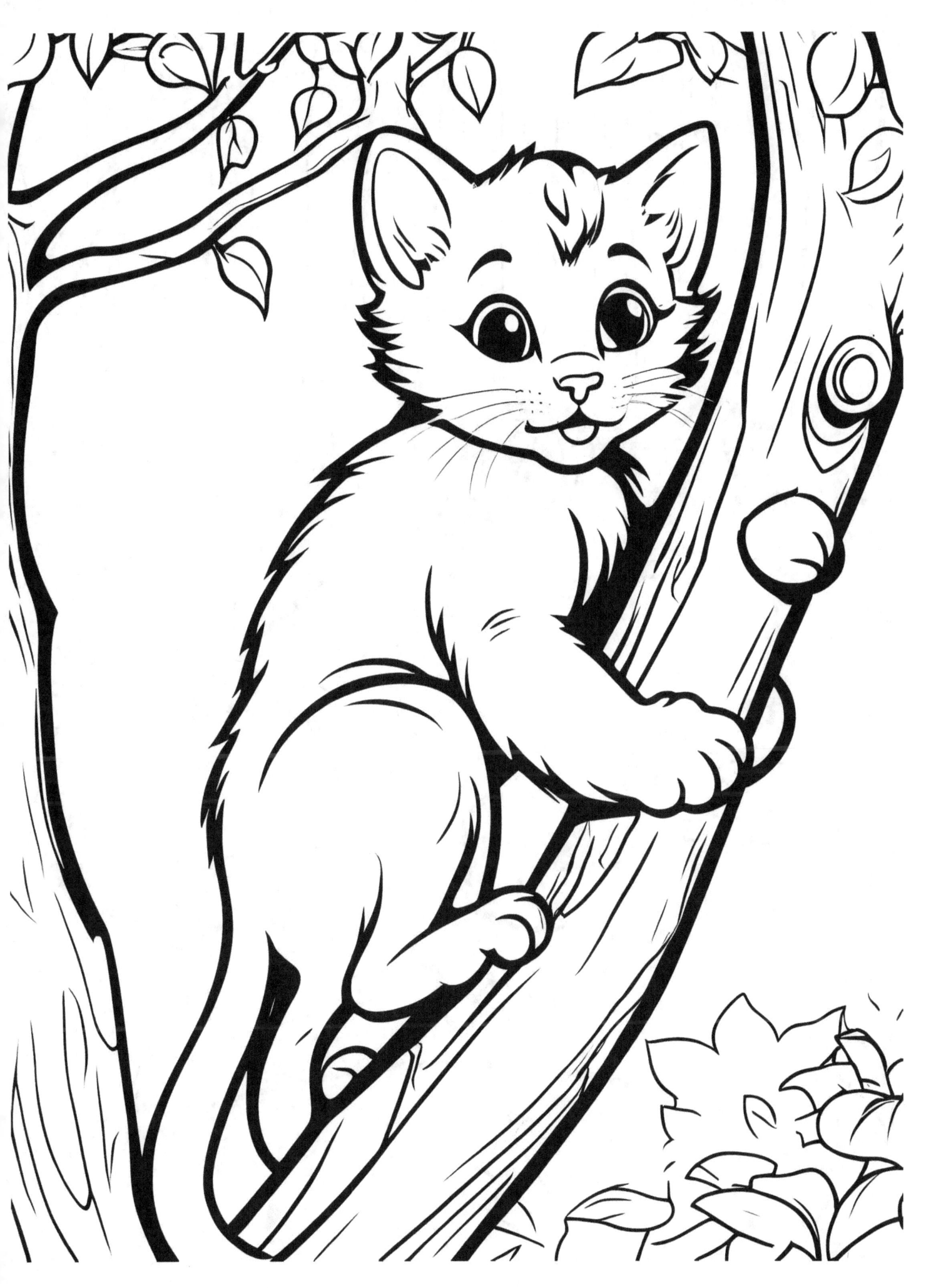

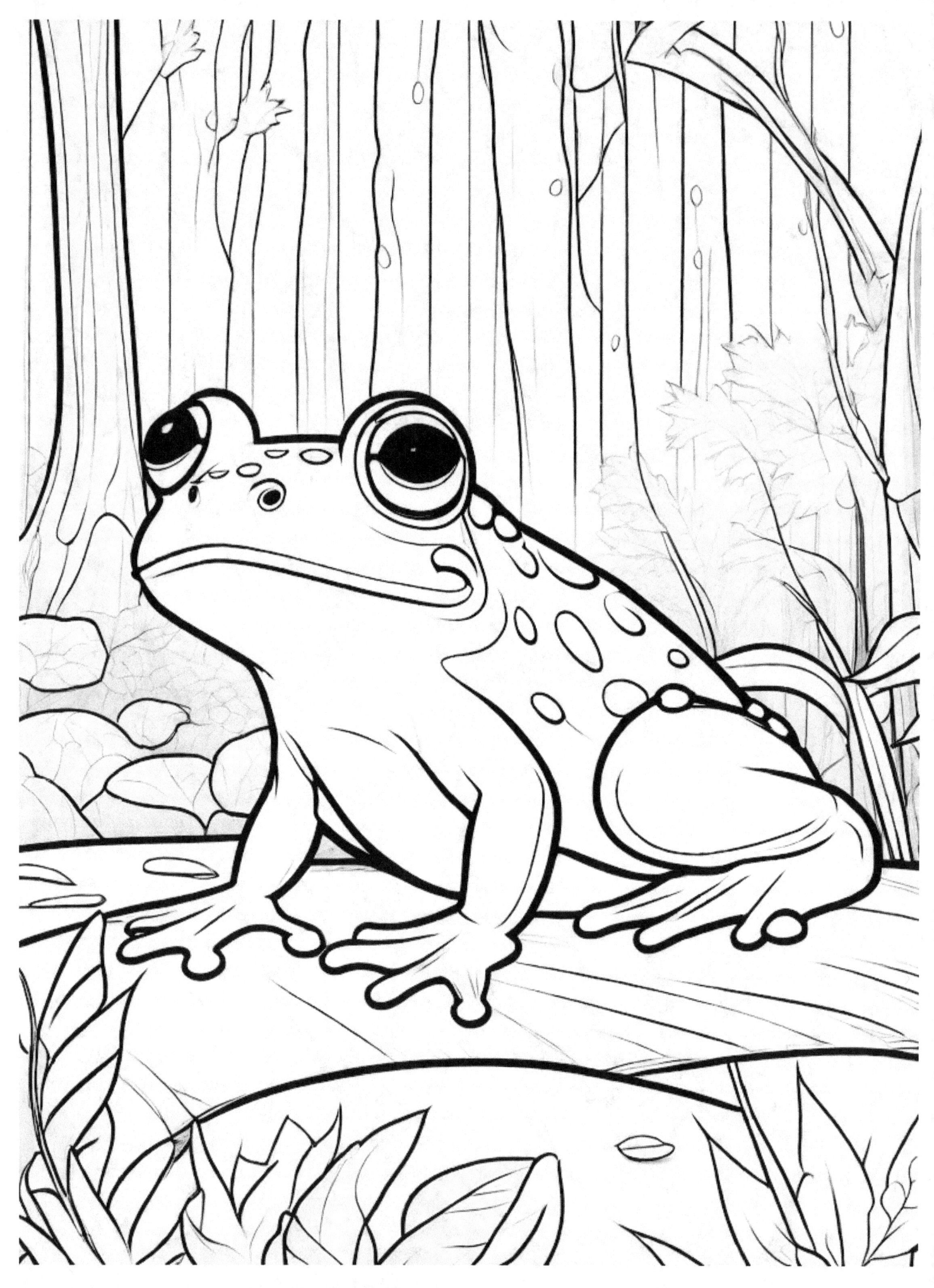

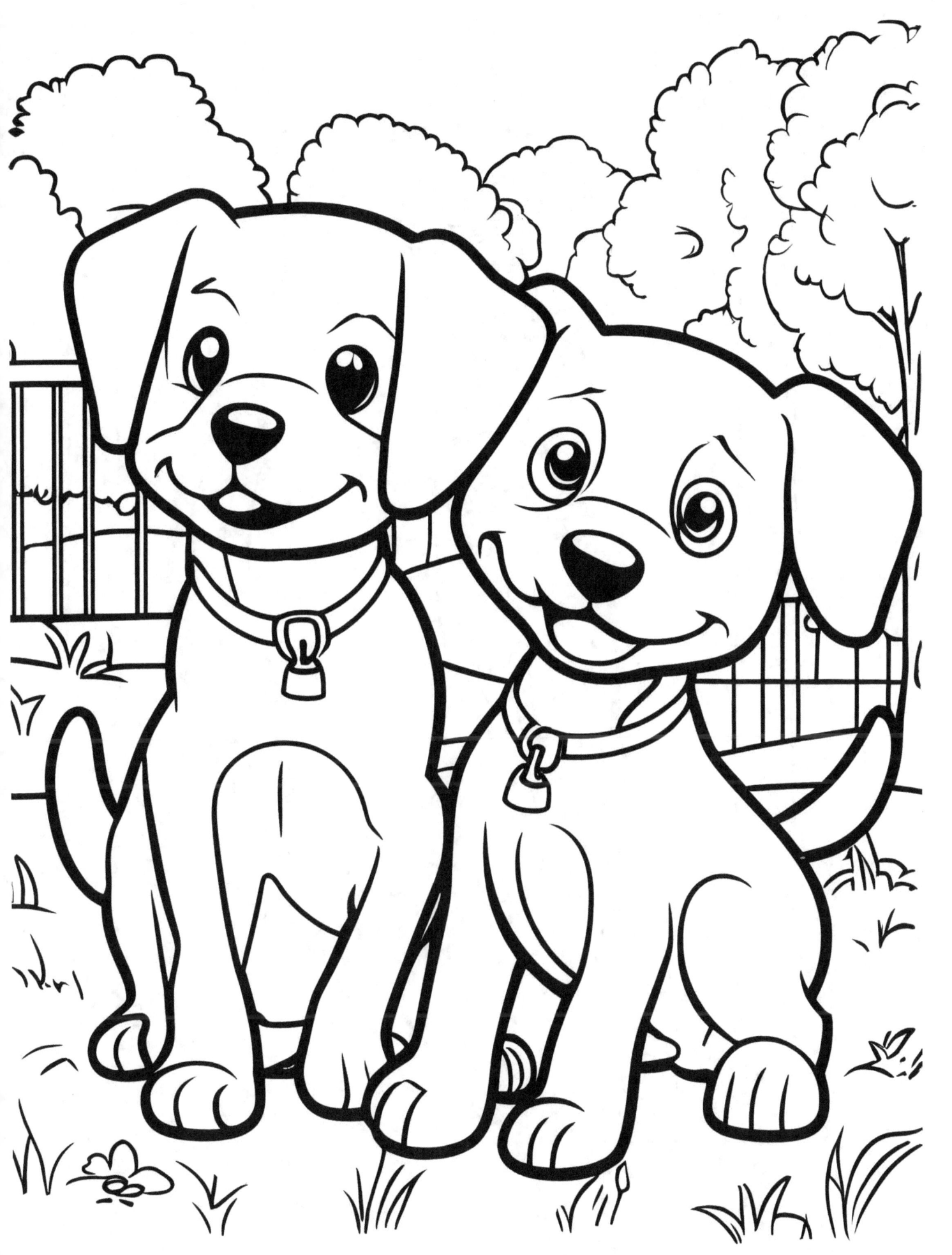

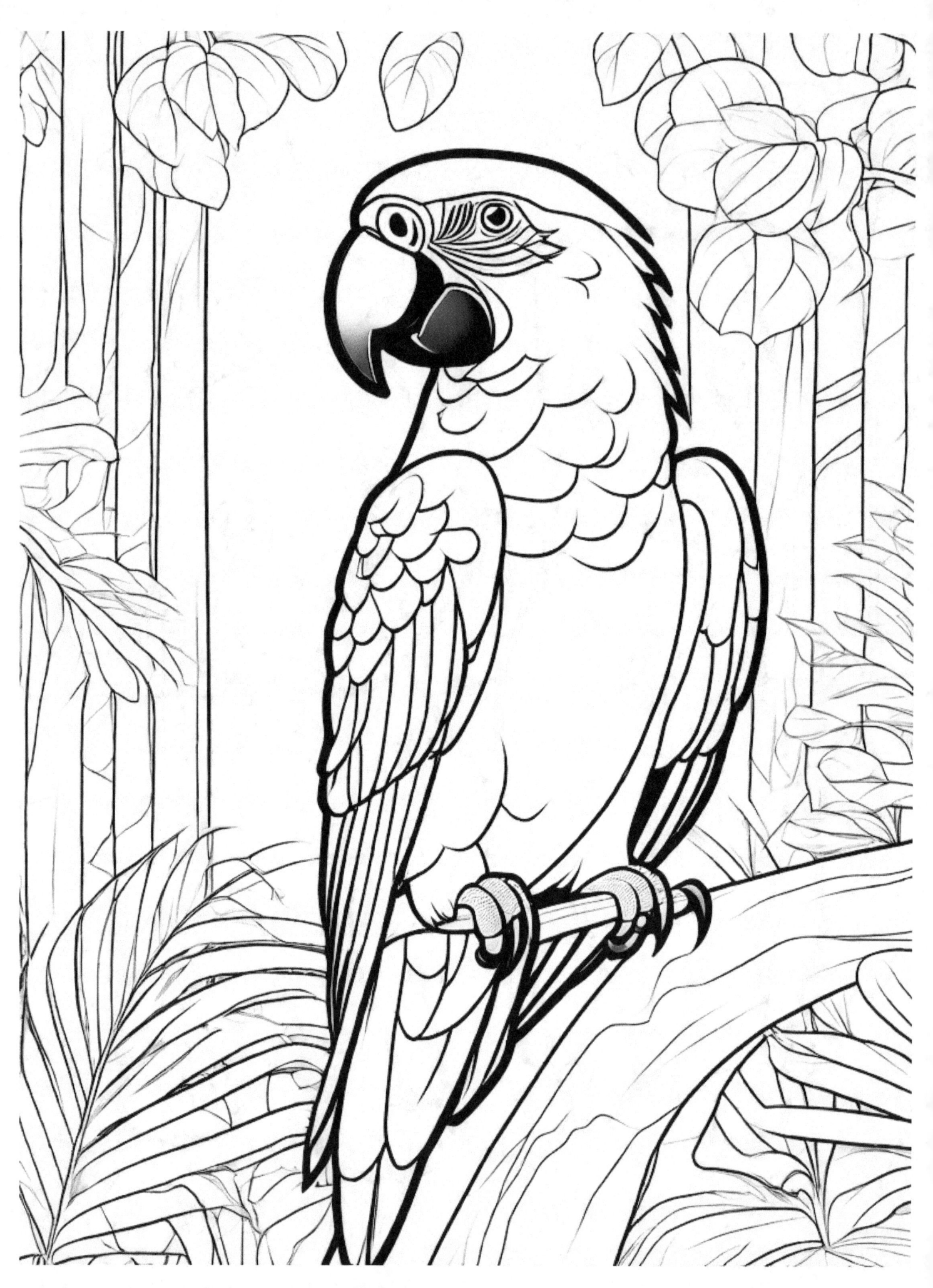

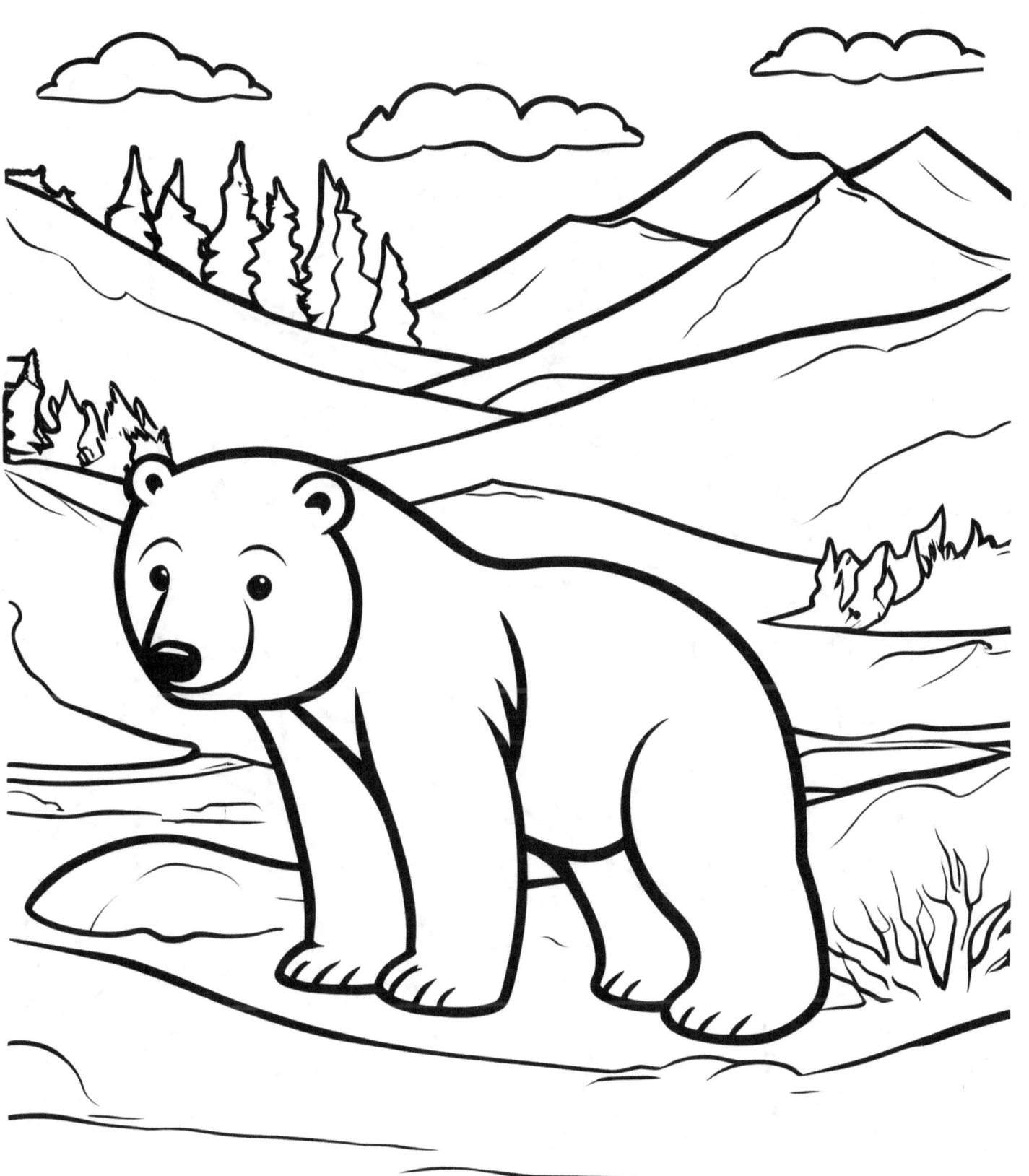

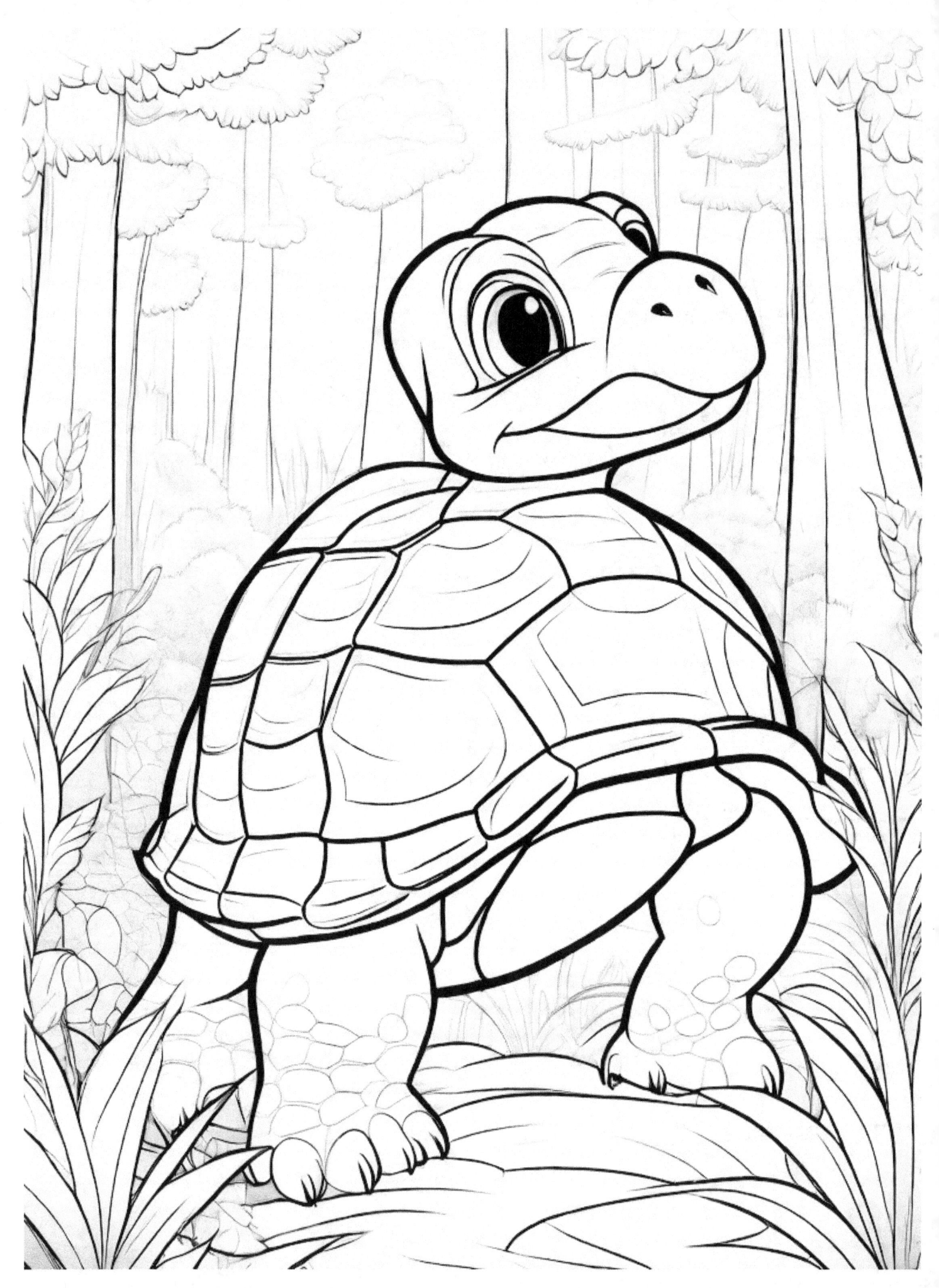

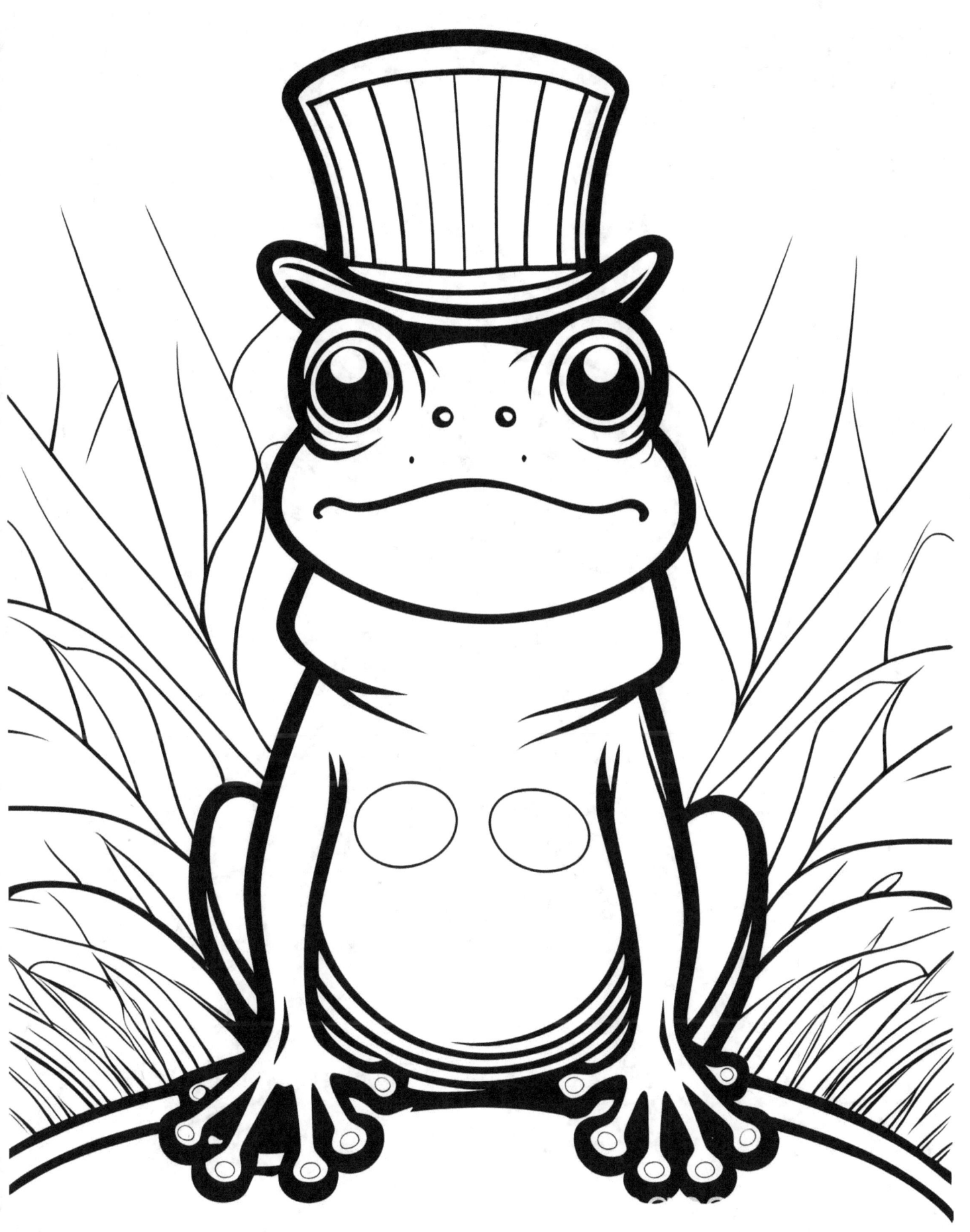

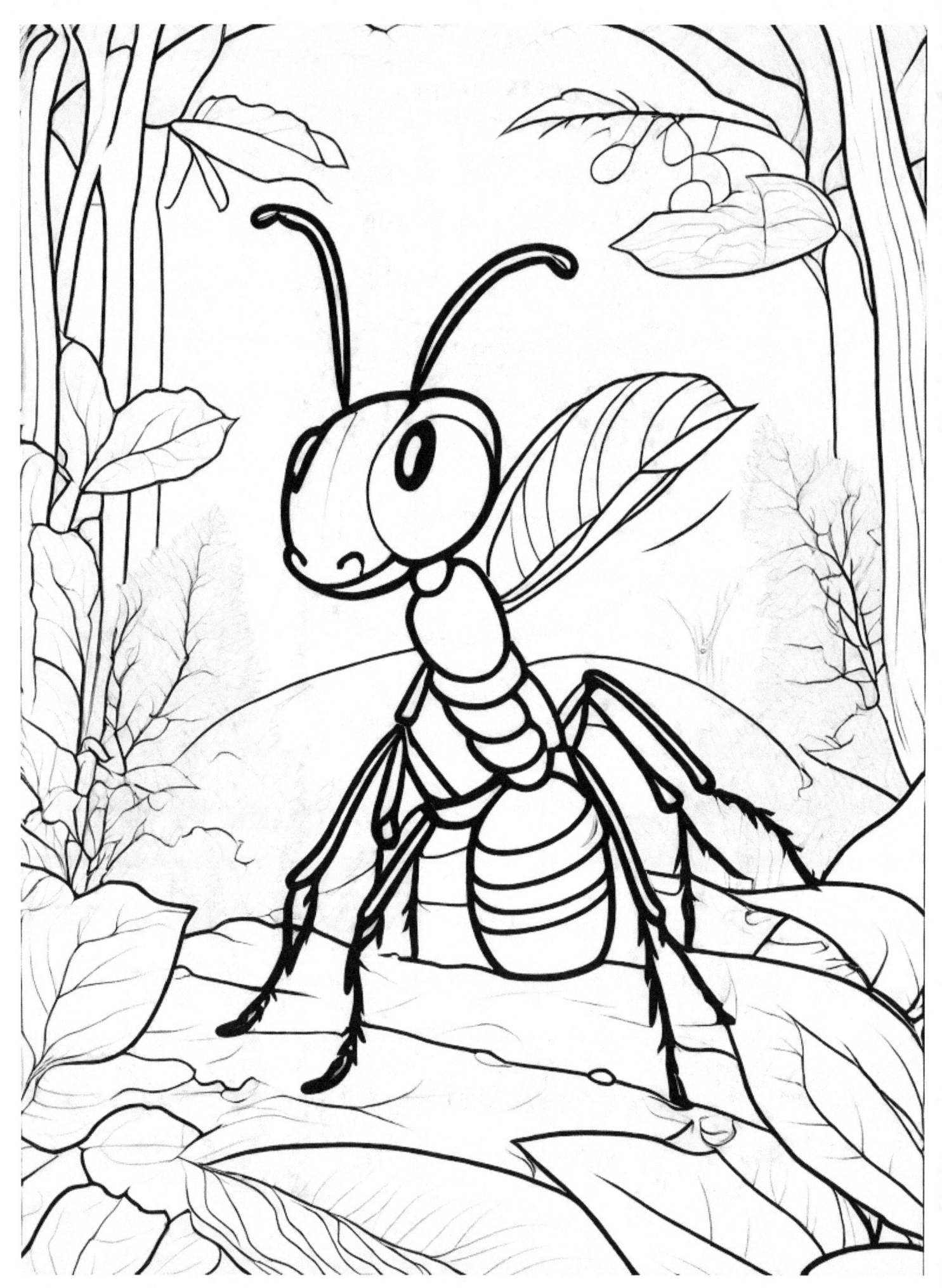

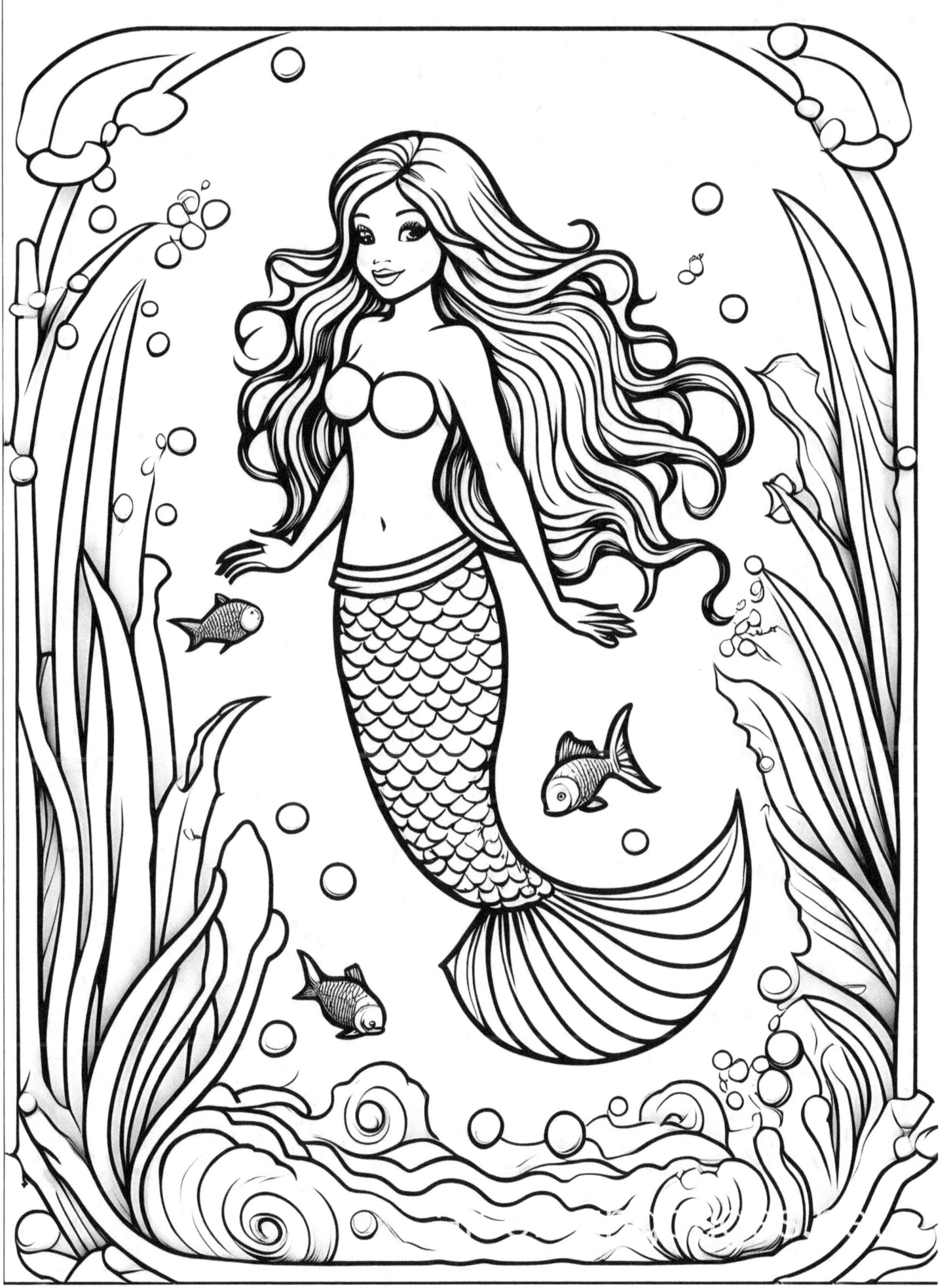

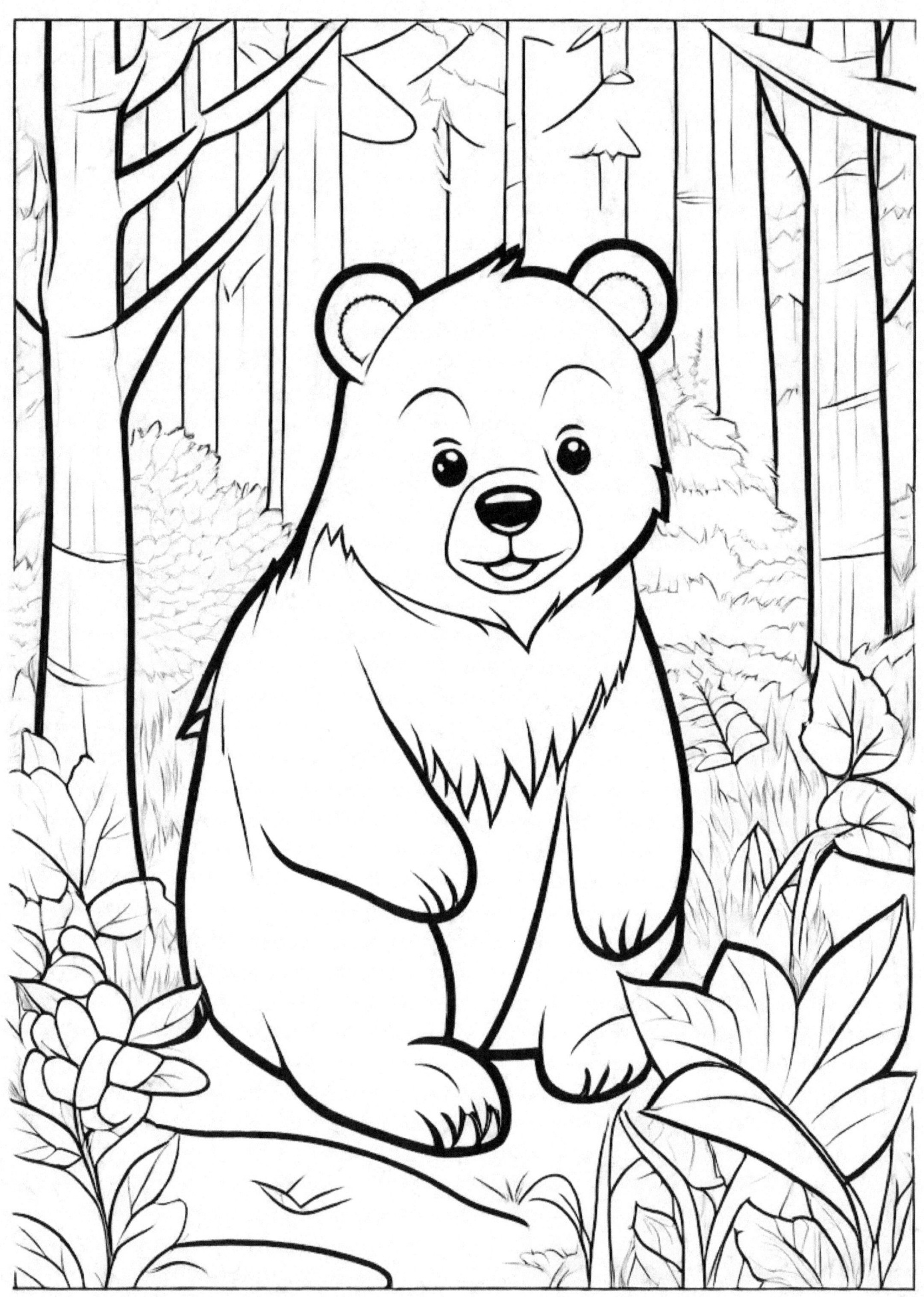

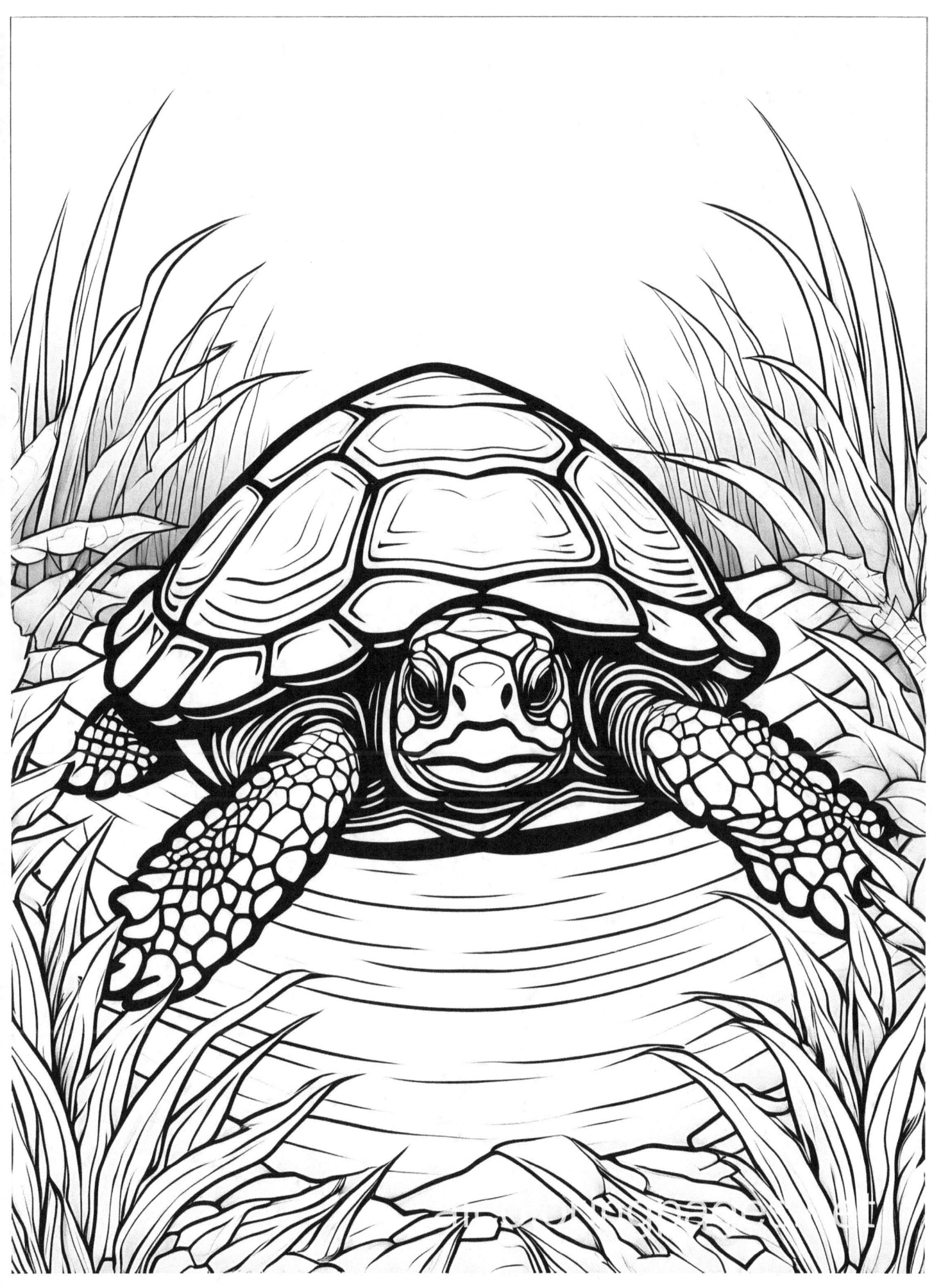

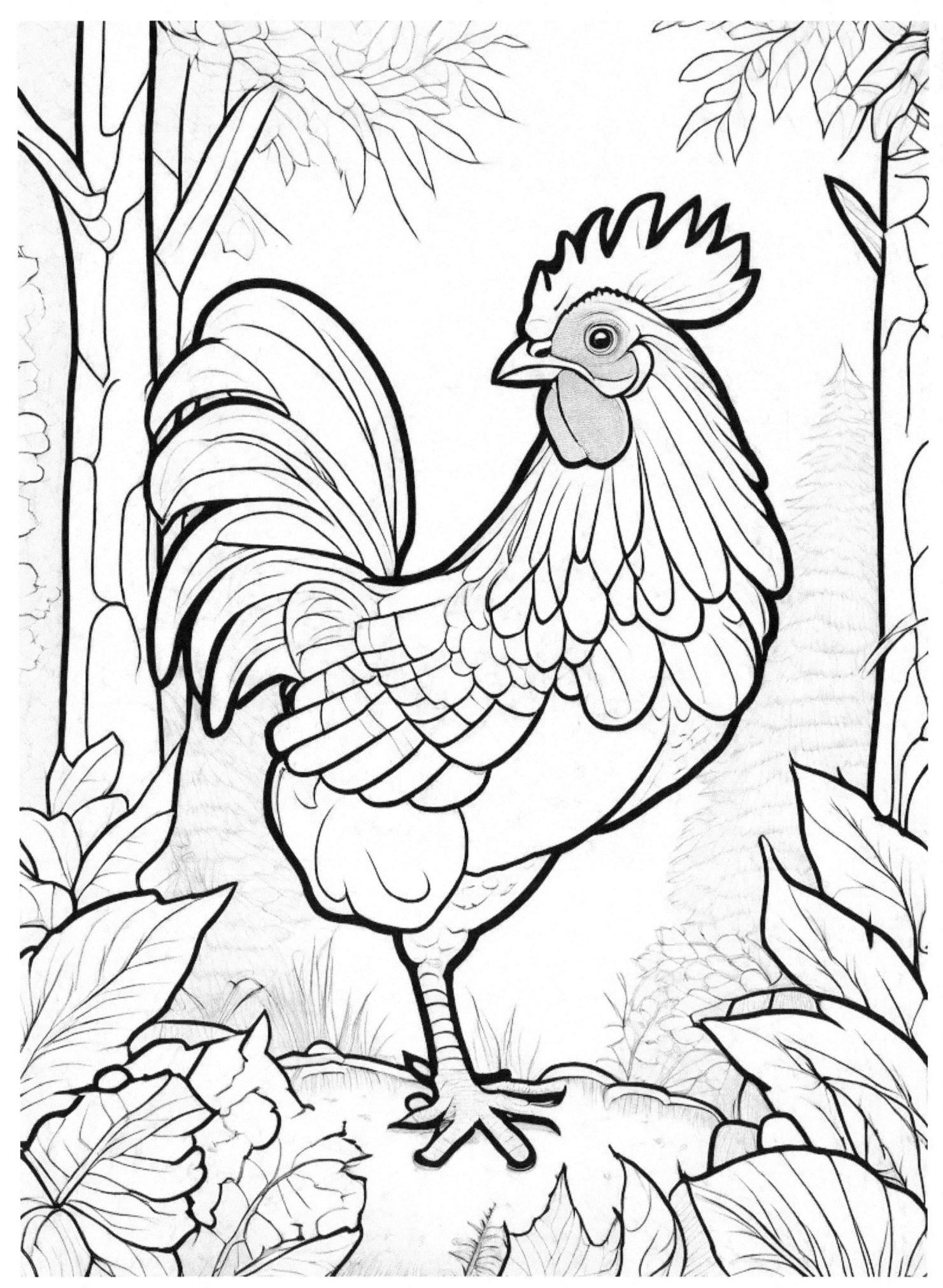

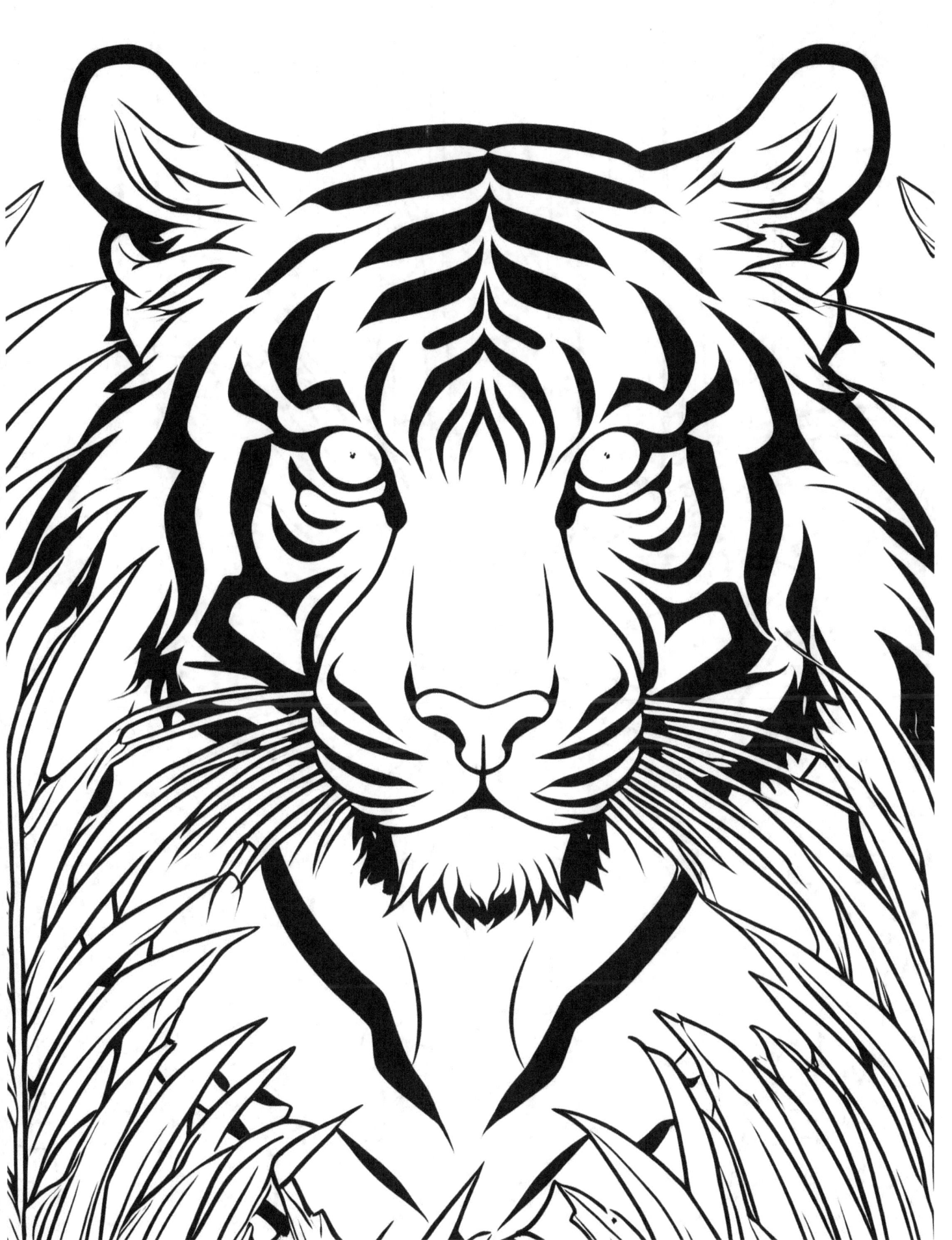

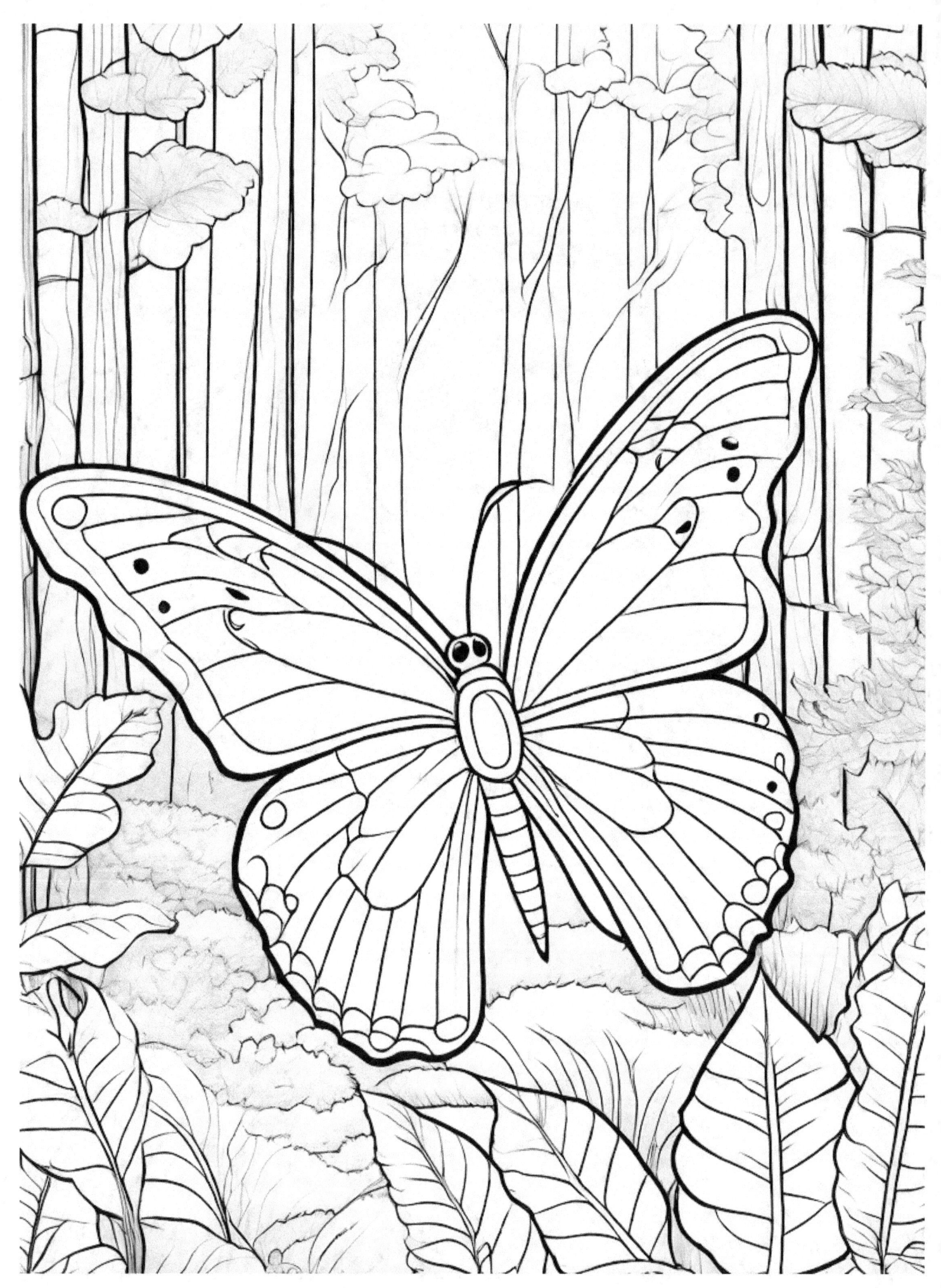

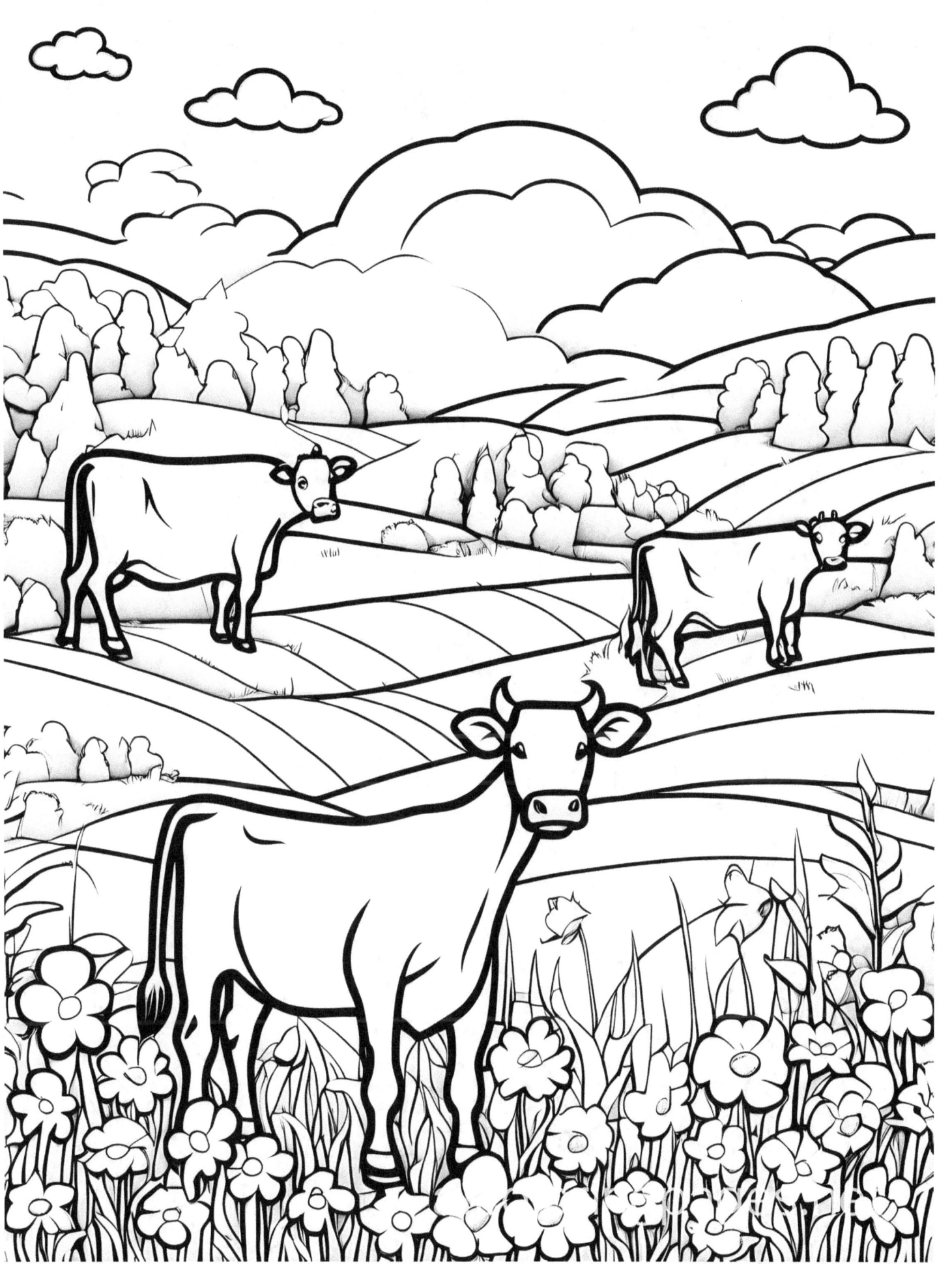

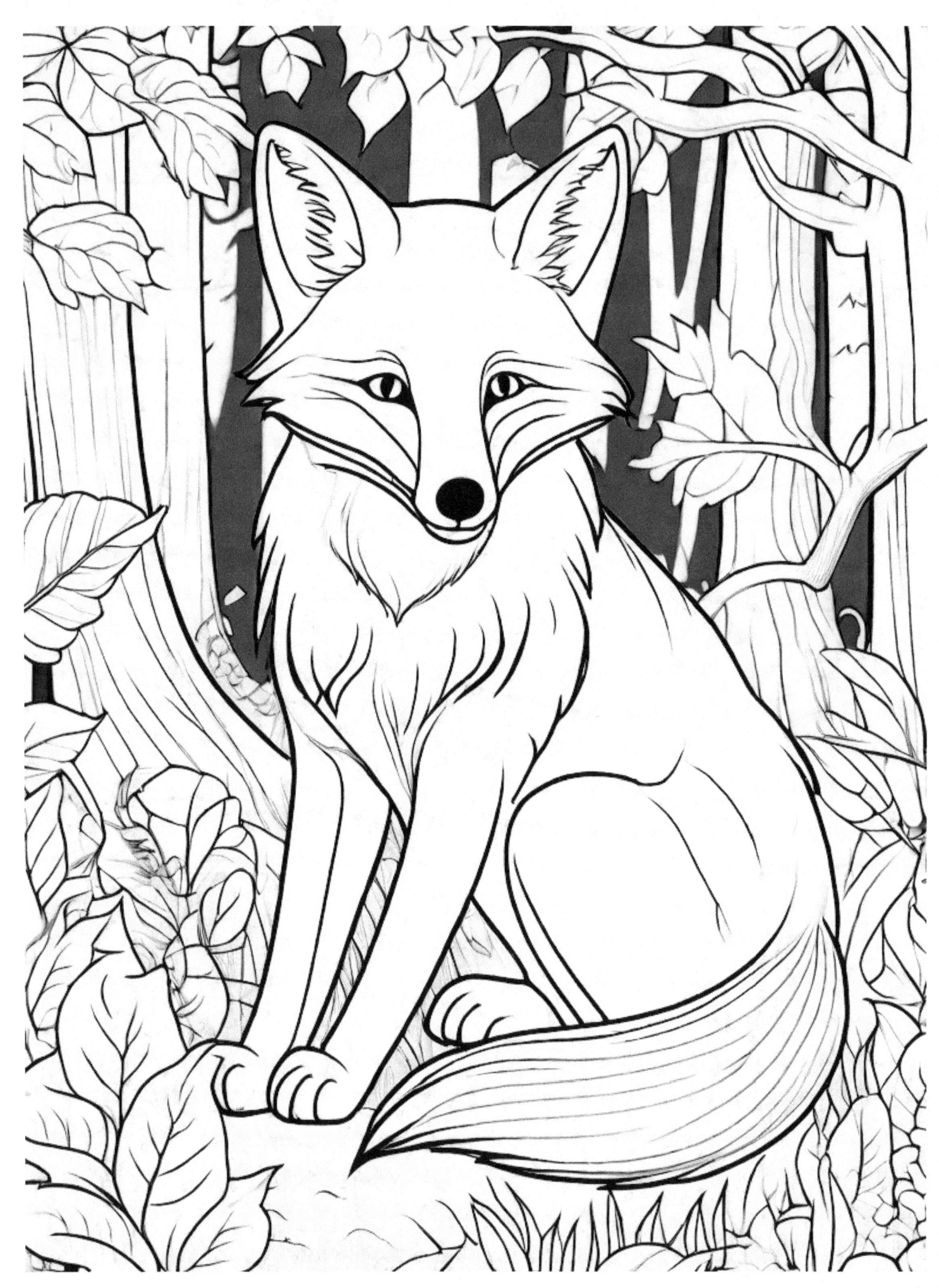

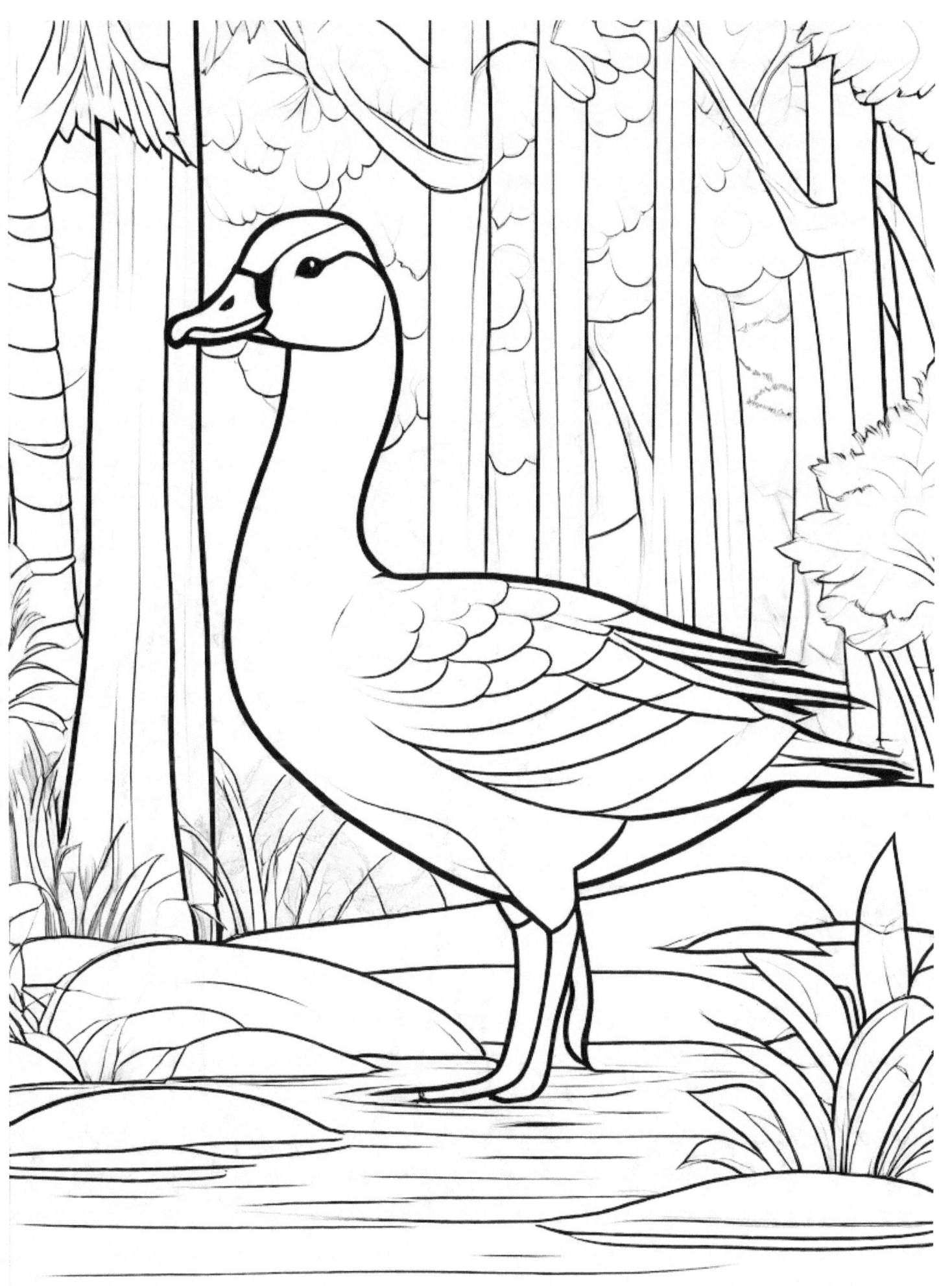

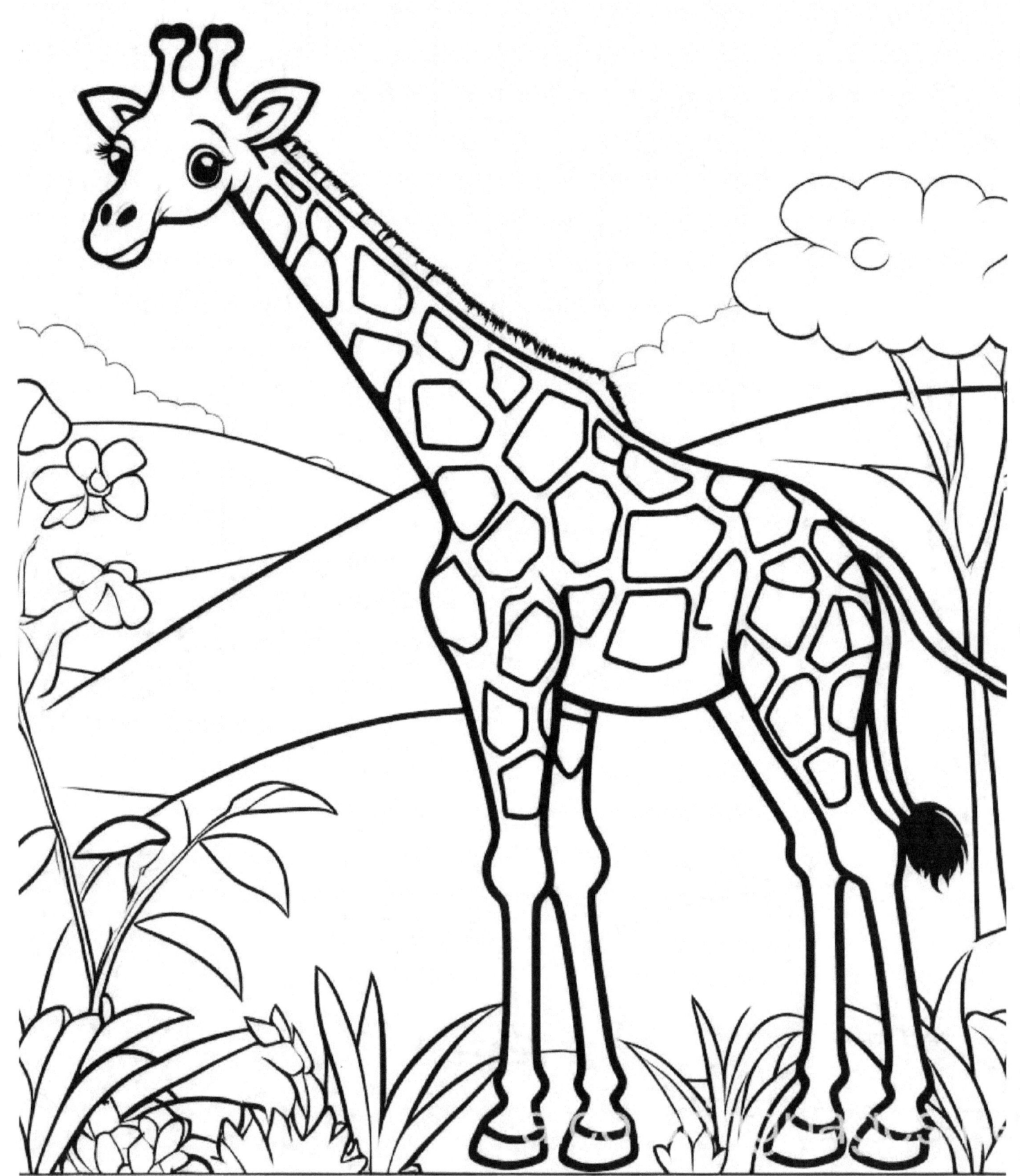

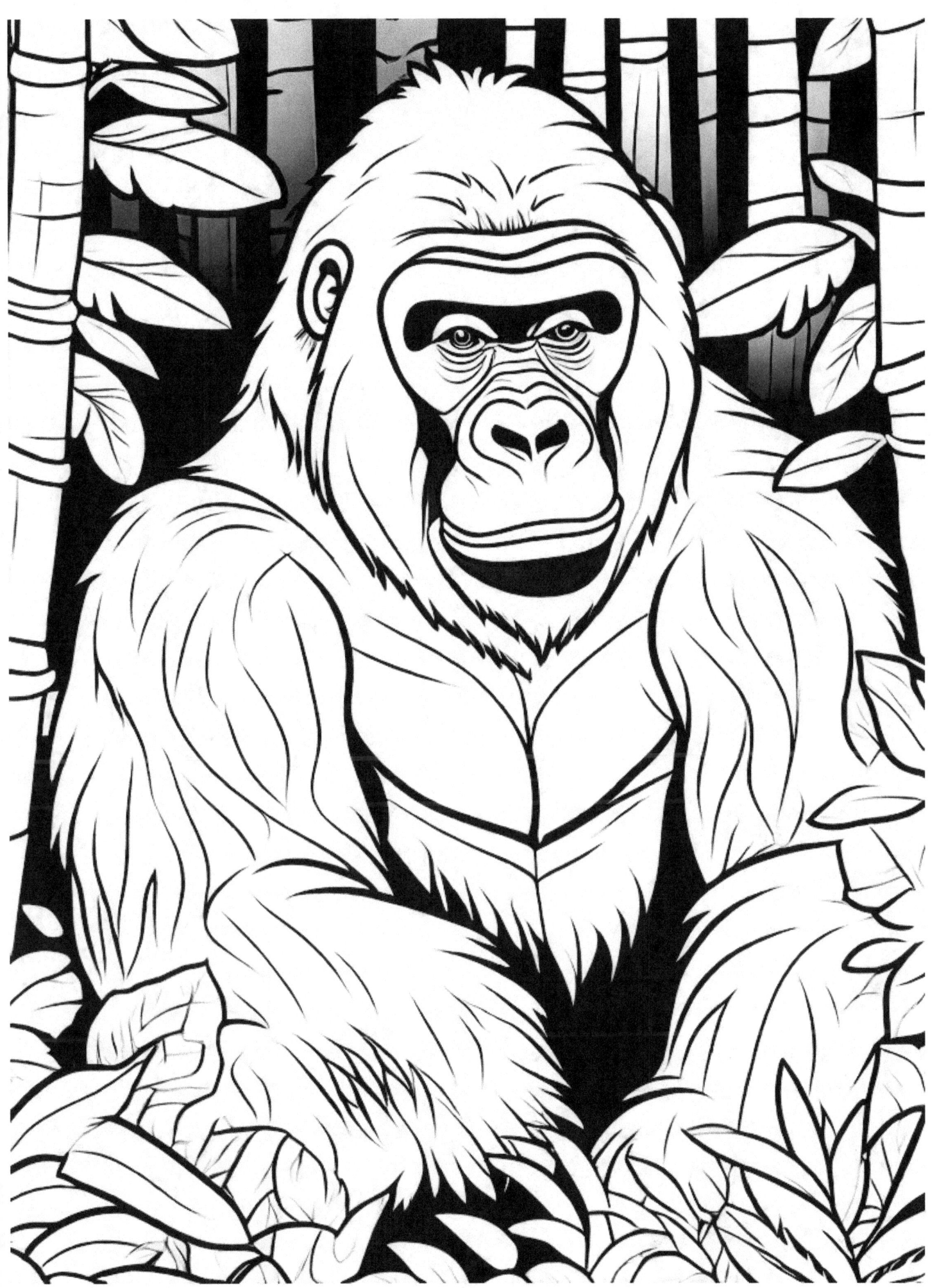

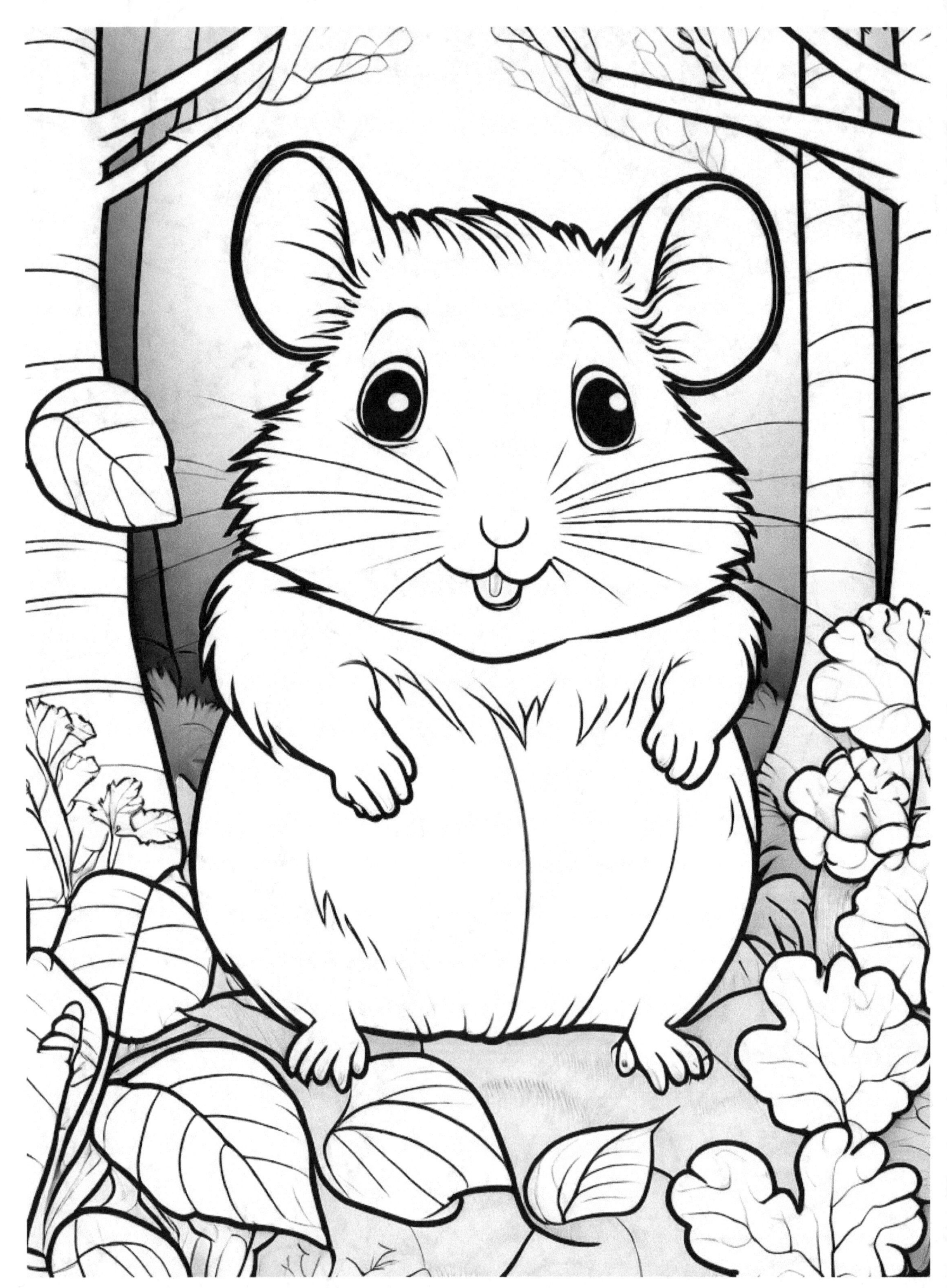

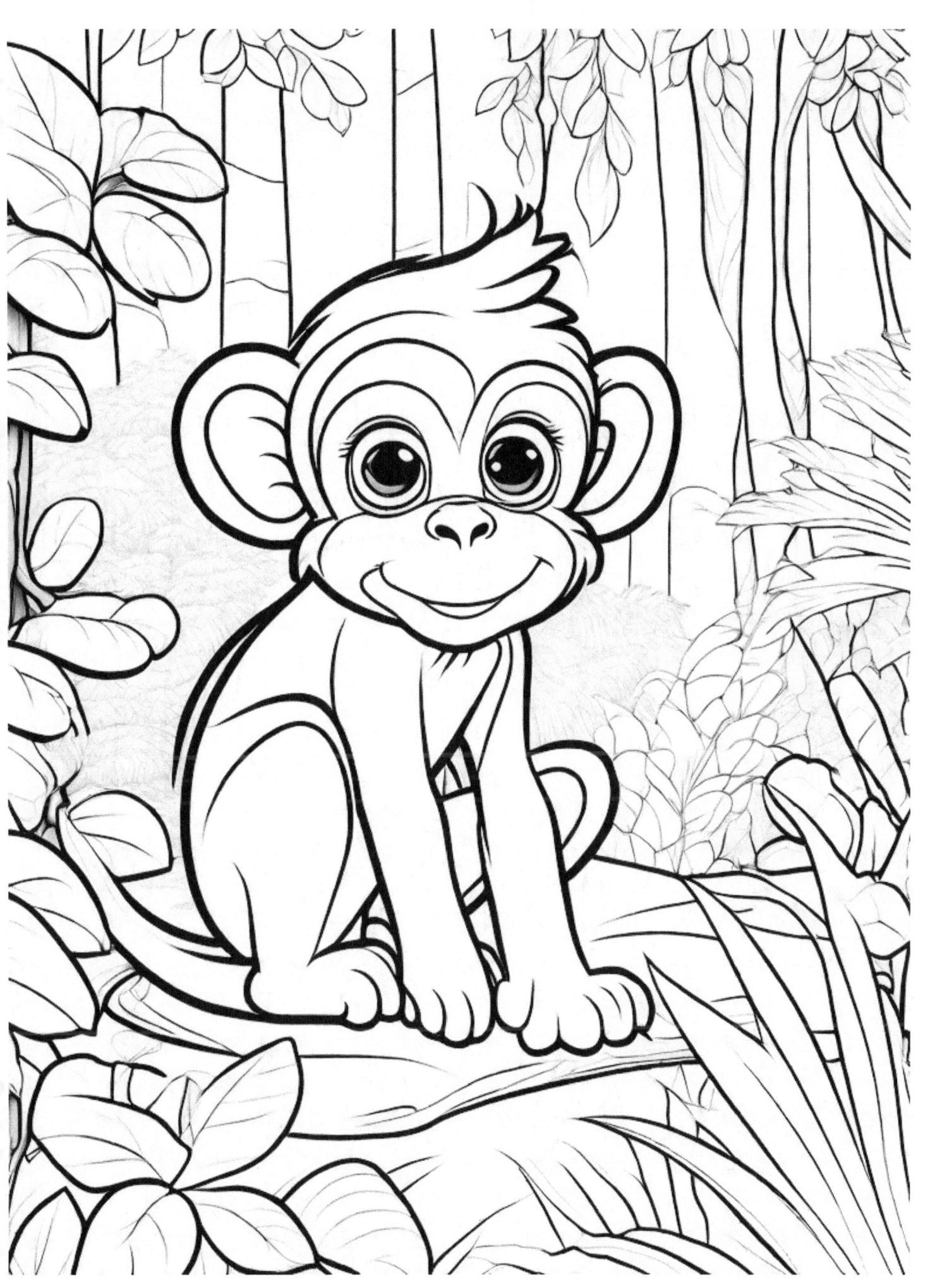

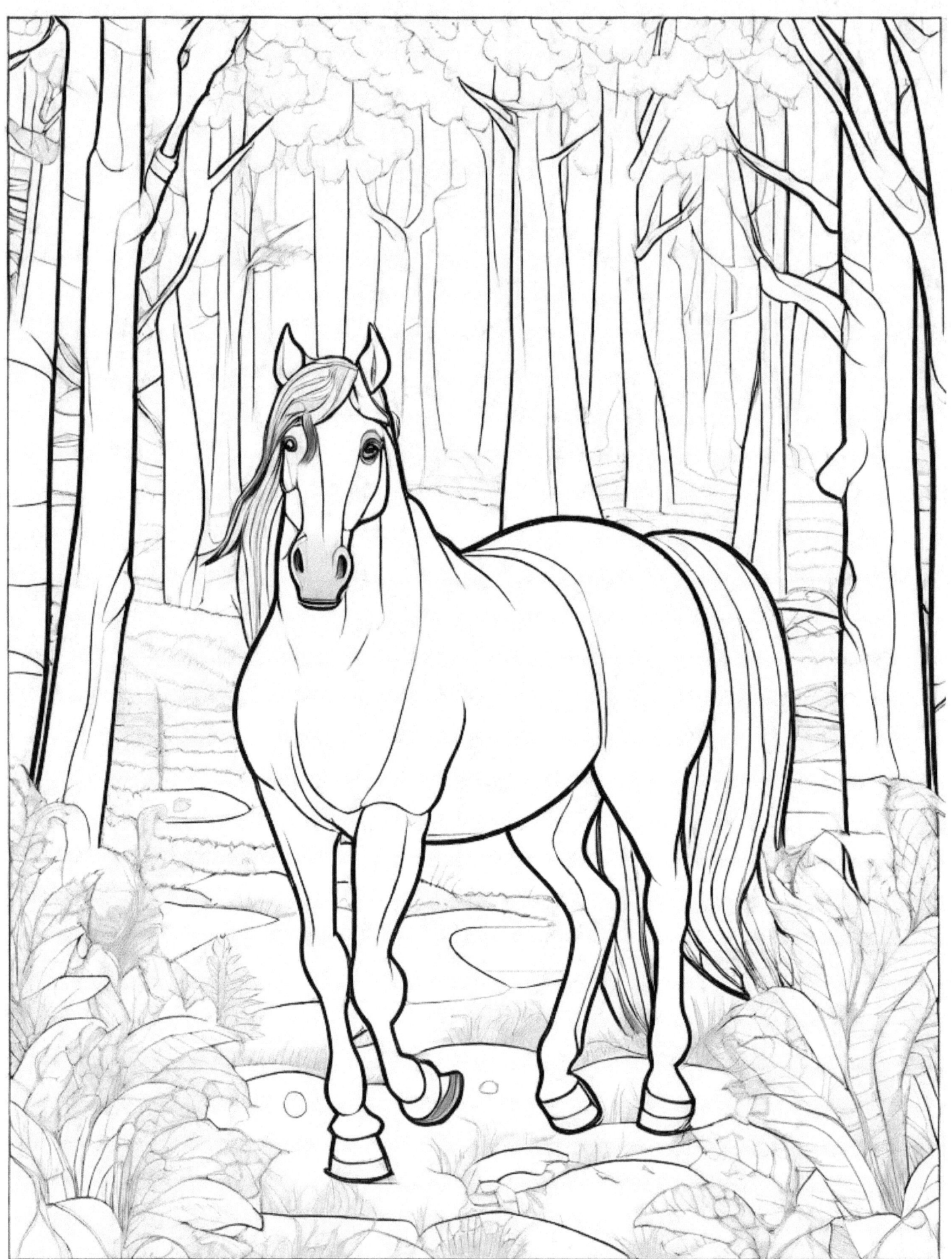

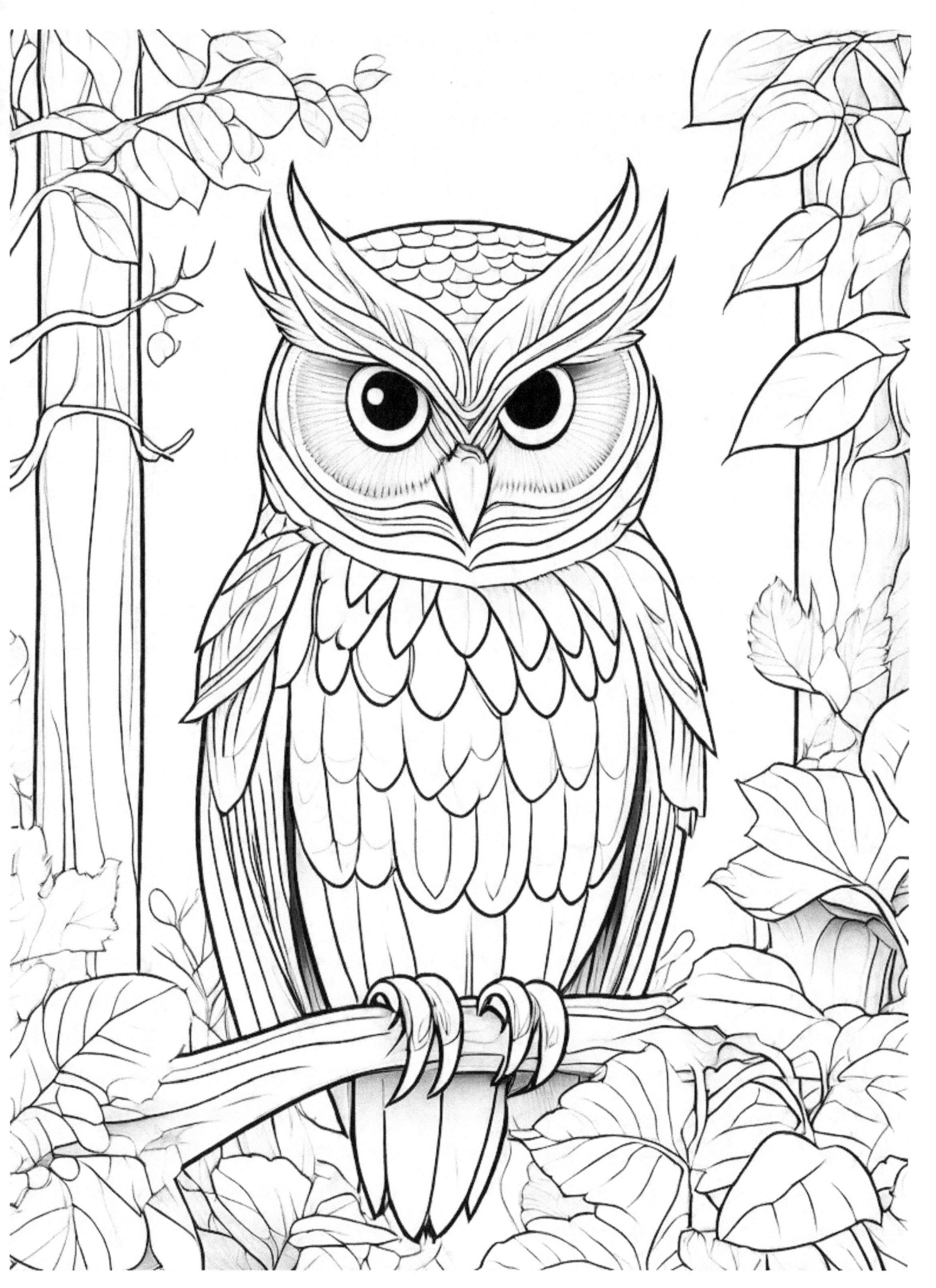

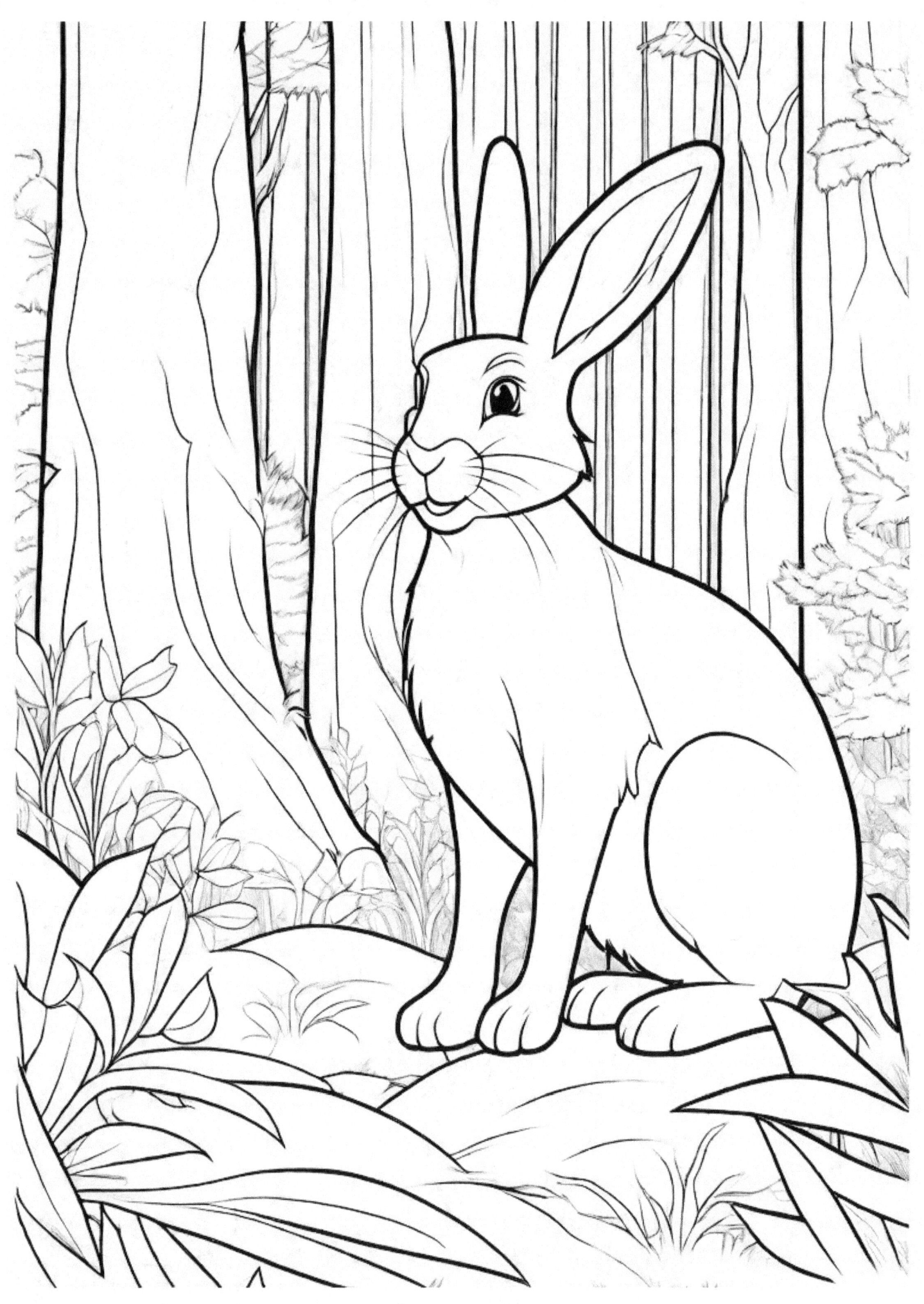

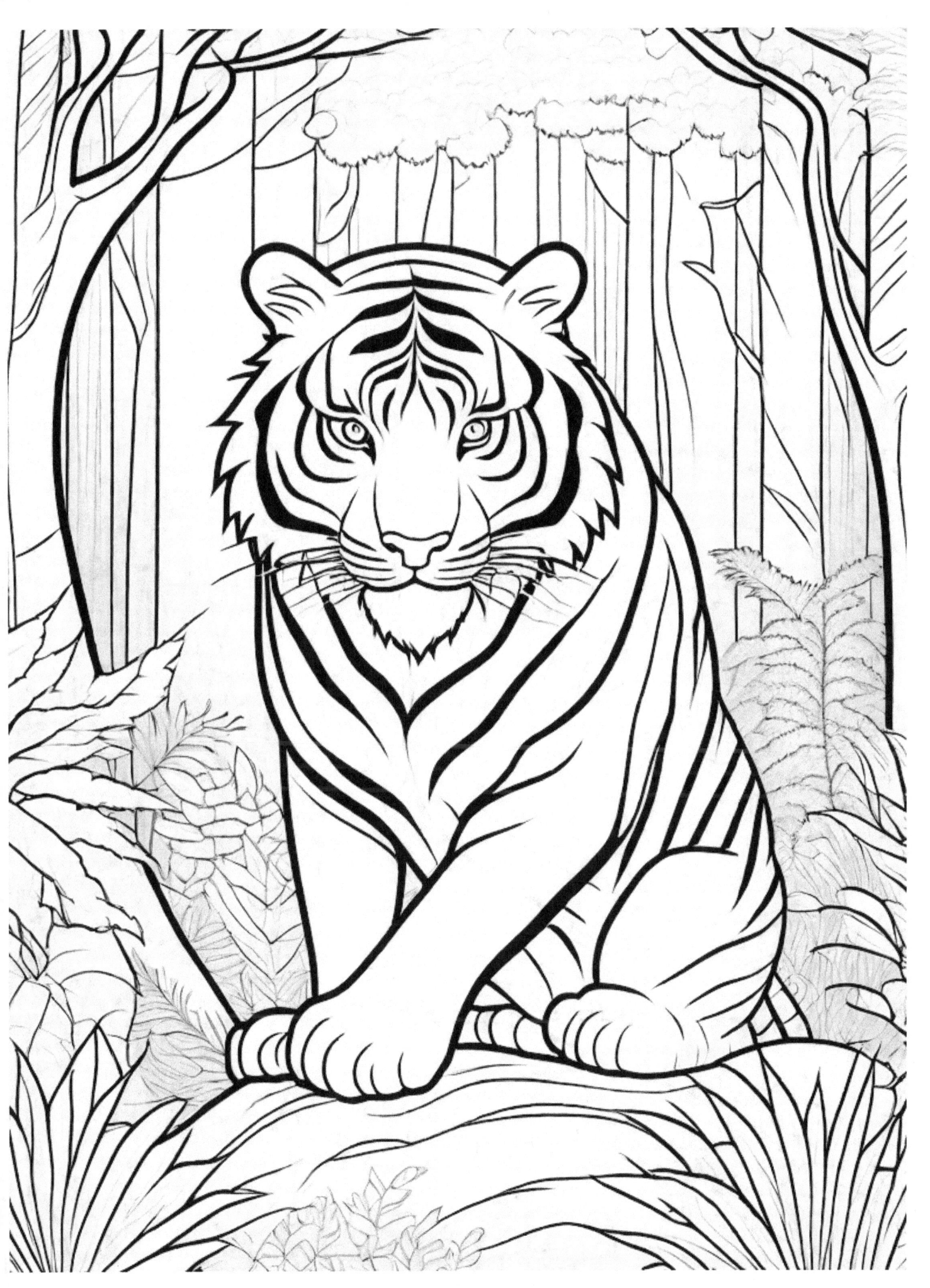

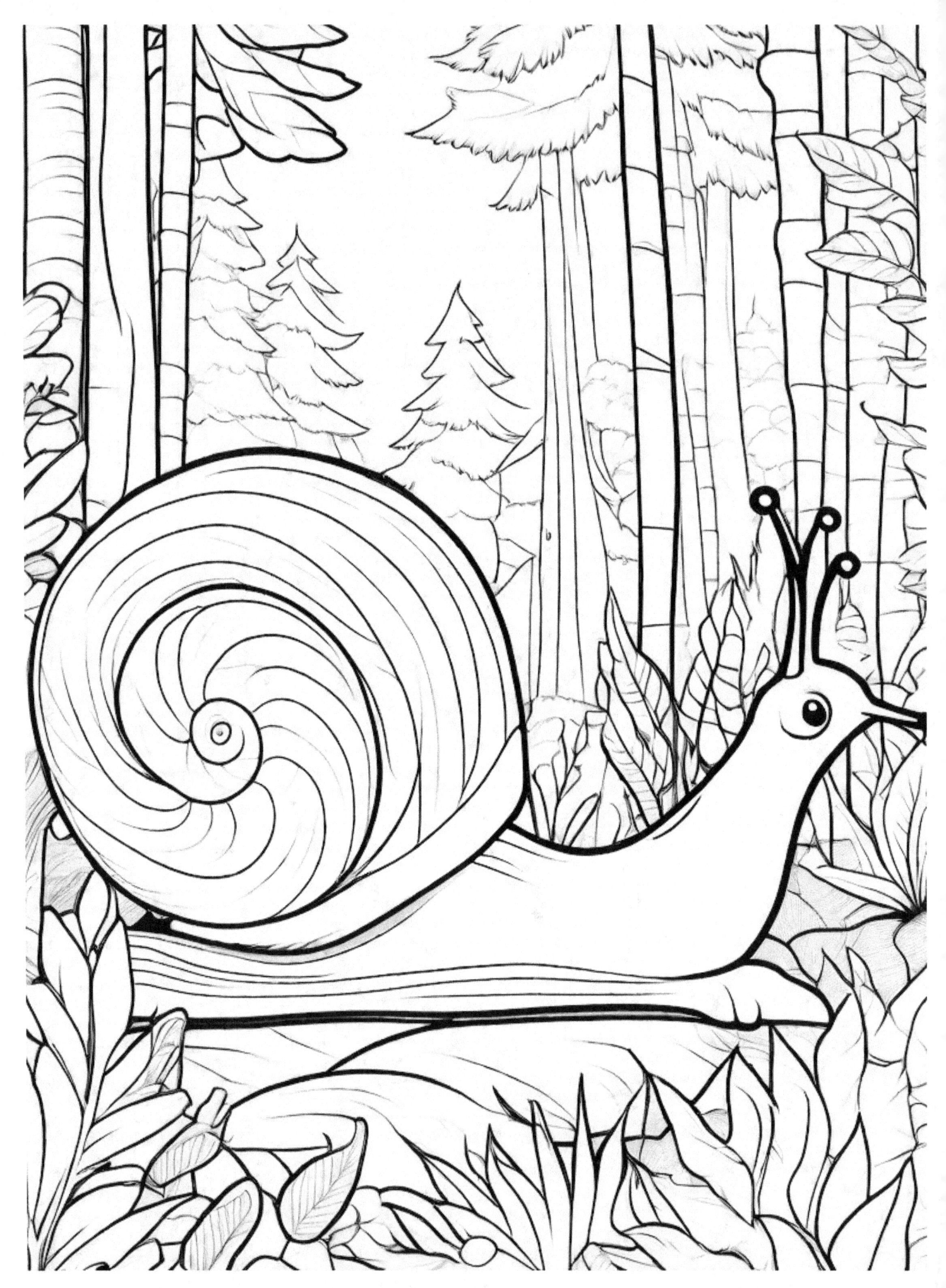

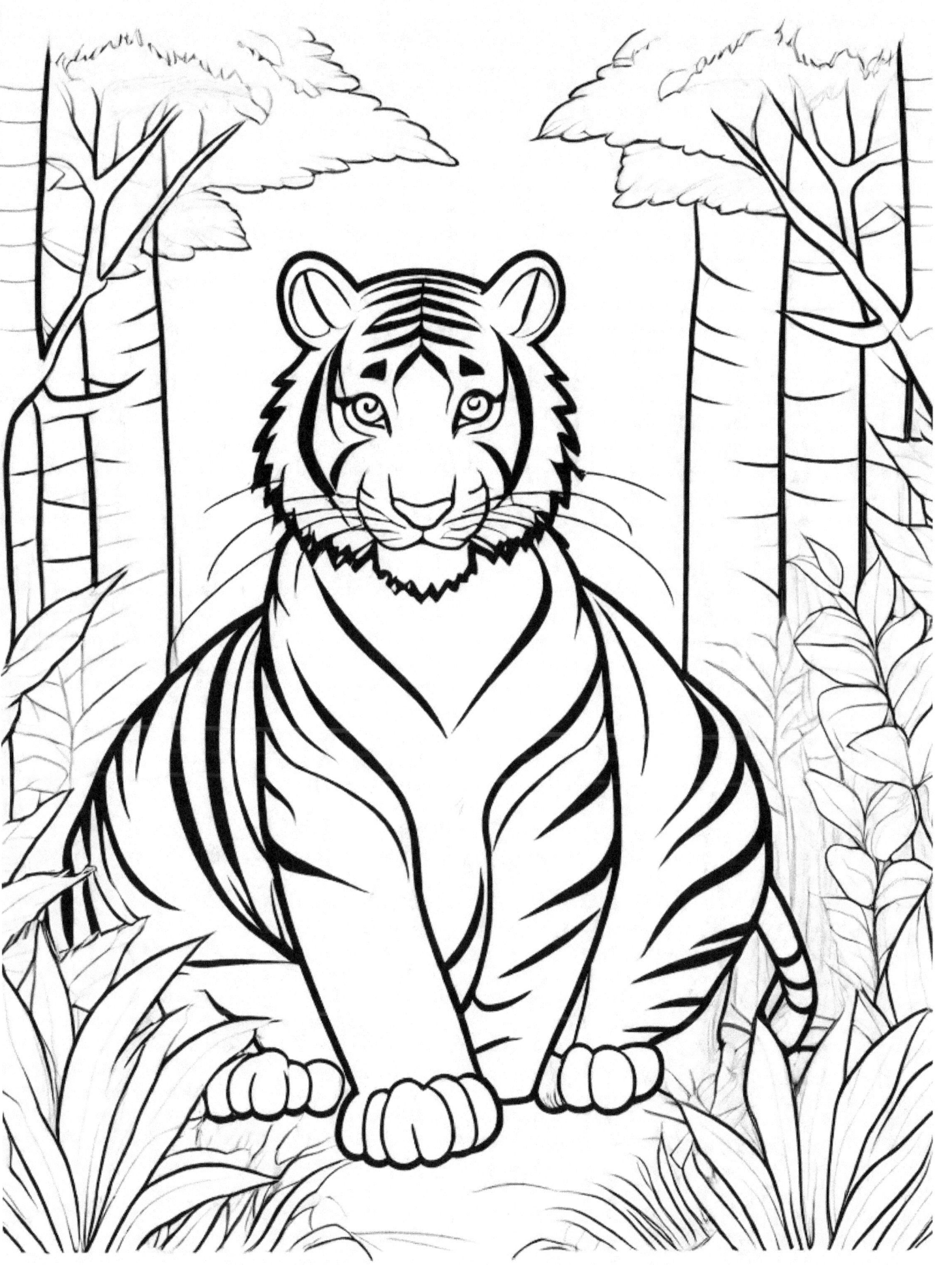

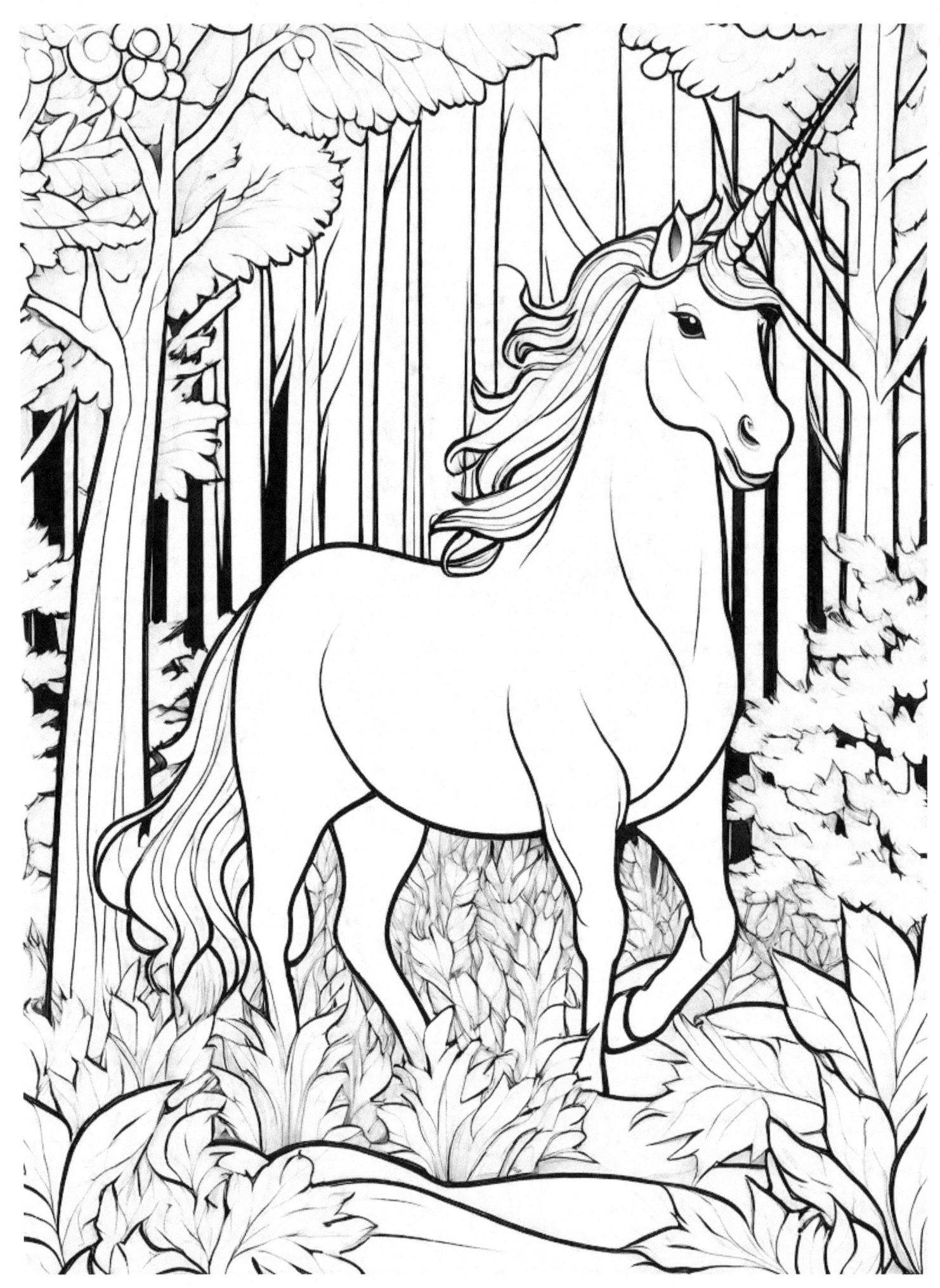

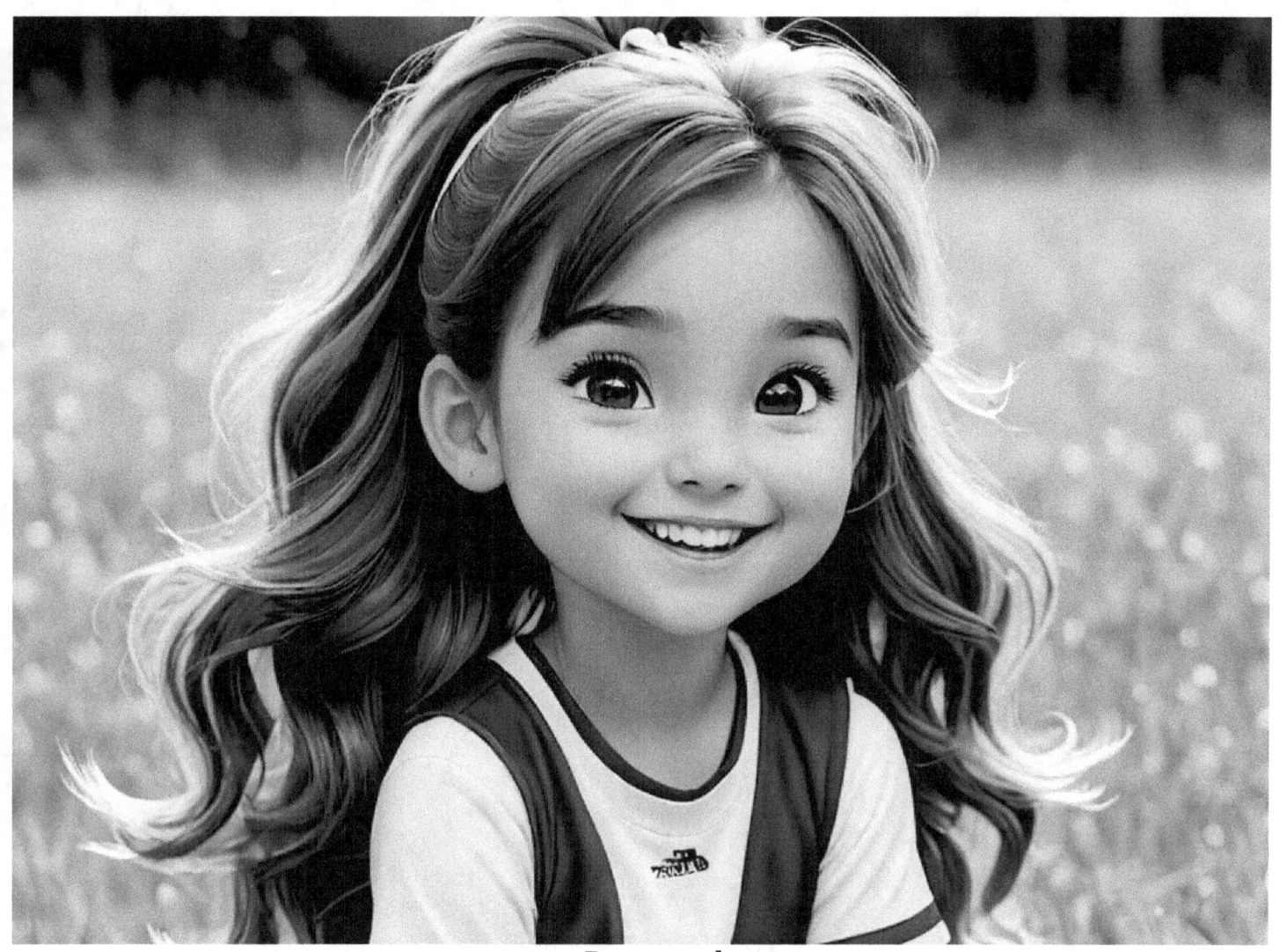

Dear reader,

Thank you very much for purchasing the coloring book and completing it. Your dedication and enthusiasm mean a lot to us. I hope you enjoyed every moment of coloring and found it a delightful experience.

As we reach the end of this book, we want to extend our gratitude for embarking on this creative journey with us. But don't worry, a new adventure awaits! Get ready to dive into the next coloring expedition, where endless possibilities and landscapes await your imagination.

Thank you again for your support and enthusiasm. Let's embark on this new adventure together!

©Di Marko publications
2024

www.ingramcontent.com/pod-product-compliance
Lightning Source LLC
Chambersburg PA
CBHW062123220526
45471CB00010B/3848